WITHDRAWN

TAKING CENTER STAGE:

Feminism in Contemporary U.S. Drama

by

JANET BROWN

The Scarecrow Press, Inc.
Metuchen, N.J., & London
1991

This book is based, in part, on the author's previous work with
Scarecrow Press, *Feminist Drama: Definition and Critical Analysis*
(1979).

British Library Cataloguing-in-Publication data available

Library of Congress Cataloging-in-Publication Data

Brown, Janet, 1952-
  Taking center stage : feminism in contemporary U.S. drama / by
Janet Brown.
      p.   cm.
  Includes bibliographical references (p.   ) and index.
  ISBN 0-8108-2448-5 (alk. paper)
    1. American drama—Women authors—History and criticism.
  2. Feminism and literature—United States—History—20th century.
  3. Feminism and theater—United States—History—20th century.
  4. Women and literature—United States—History—20th century.
  5. American drama—20th century—History and criticism.   I. Title.
PS338.F45B7   1991
812'.509352042—dc20   91-23952

Contents

Acknowledgments

I would like to acknowledge the support of the Women's Research Institute of Hartford College for Women. By appointing me a research associate, the Institute gave me access to its excellent library of women's studies materials and to its superlative librarians.

Without the patient, critical readings of Sandy Nickel and Catherine Stevenson, this manuscript could not have been completed. Without their faithful friendship, it would not have been begun.

I thank my daughter, Molly Brown Reuter, who helpfully napped through much of this book's creation, and who spent the rest of the time playing in the next room with her favorite babysitter, Carl Haslinger, when they were one year old and twelve years old respectively. Together, Molly and Carl offered me more than time to write. They offered me an inspiring vision of the brave, gentle women and men of the future.

Last and first, I thank my husband, Paul Reuter. With a marriage partner like Paul, I can never lose heart that women and men will find ways to work it out.

JANET BROWN
Hartford, CT

1 • Introduction

In 1977, I proposed a doctoral dissertation on the subject of feminist drama. My attempted review of the literature, a requisite first step, revealed that almost nothing had been written on the subject. Indeed, while a great deal of feminist literary, rhetorical, and social criticism had already been produced, a definition of a concept as essential as feminism itself was not easily obtained. In the end, I quoted Simone de Beauvoir, Gerda Lerner, and Aileen S. Kraditor in producing a simple and (I hoped) inarguable definition: I defined feminism as woman's quest for autonomy in a patriarchal society.

My method of analysis was based on Kenneth Burke's "dramatistic" approach to literature. Burke posits that every work of literature is a symbolic act with a rhetorical intention. In Burke's system, every literary work (and indeed every historical event) can be analyzed in terms of the relationships among five basic elements: Agent, Act, Agency, Scene, and Purpose. These terms combine to form a drama, or action, which is a paradigm of history. The initial state in this drama is an ordered hierarchy. Then an agent disobeys this hierarchy, experiences guilt, and dreams of salvation, of a more perfect order than the present one. Redemption, however, requires a redeemer, a victim. If the drama ends in victimization, a scapegoat is sacrificed for the sake of the new order. If the end is mortification, in the order of perfect love, the agent may voluntarily sacrifice him/herself for the sake of the new order (Leland Griffin, 457-458).

The pentad operates as a means of analyzing the pattern of symbolic action. One first determines what the five terms are in a particular work or event, and then which of the relation-

ships among the terms is the most revealing of the pattern of
symbolic action. The definition of feminist drama I employed
featured as agent a woman. Her act would be to seek autonomy, and the scene would be a patriarchal society. The relationship among these three terms would reveal the play's pattern
of symbolic action.

Because of its focus on rhetorical motive, Burkean method-
ology seemed especially appropriate to the analysis of feminist
work. Describing his approach to analysis, Burke said, "It
assumes that a poem's [or a play's] structure is to be described
most accurately by thinking always of the poem's function. It
assumes that the poem is designed to 'do something' for the
poet and his [/her] readers, and that we can make the most
relevant observations about its design by considering the
poem as the embodiment of this act" (75). Also, and just as
important to me then, Burke is a respected male literary critic
under whose aegis I was able to win the approval of my
dissertation committee for a thesis on the (then) questionable
topic of feminist drama.

But my definition, which had seemed quite encompassing
in 1977, had become somewhat constraining by 1979 when
the book based on my dissertation appeared. Burke is certainly correct in noting that the symbolic pattern of an unjust
society absolved by the sacrifice of a scapegoat has permeated
Western history and literature. But already in 1979, as I noted
then, feminist theorists such as Mary Daly had condemned
this very pattern of symbolic action for providing sexist
society with a justification for the oppression of women. At
the same time, plays such as Susan Griffin's *Voices* and Ntozake
Shange's *For Colored Girls Who Have Considered Suicide When
the Rainbow Is Enuf* had begun to appear, plays with a communal protagonist and without a single dominant narrative line,
plays in which nothing traditionally "dramatic" ever happens,
but plays with clearly feminist themes. A definition that
presumed a single agent performing a significant public act
before a faceless community now appeared not untrue, but
not always to the point, either.

In the last decade, plays by and/or about women have appeared on the commercial stage in unprecedented numbers, reflecting a variety of structures and points of view. Plays depicting a woman's struggle for autonomy have continued to appear, reflecting, perhaps, liberal feminism's assumption (and my own, initially) that a woman's story in Western culture will be like a man's—when it is allowed to be told. Plays with communal female protagonists, as Honor Moore has noted, have become so common that they nearly constitute a genre of their own, but a genre ranging widely in substance and style, and one employed by male playwrights as well as by females.

Can this wealth of drama be said to have feminism (or anything else, for that matter) in common? This time, I have attempted to answer this question by taking an approach that is inductive at first. That is, in close textual analysis of a limited number of plays, I have searched for evidence of both a distinctly female narrative structure and a distinctively feminist rhetorical intention. Then, I have attempted to relate the themes, structures, and values uncovered in this search with the work of feminist theorists and scholars in the same time period.

To my knowledge, such an attempt has not been made prior to my own. Anthologies and historical surveys have, however, appeared, some of which speculate in general terms on these questions. Chinoy and Jenkins, editors of *Women in American Theatre,* offer an anthology of historical essays. They note that a recurrent theme in the lives of the women profiled is a devotion to artistic vision rather than to the commercial aspects of theatre:

> From the female shaman . . . to the Broadway star . . . to the feminist activists . . . this large vision has shaped the role of women in American theatre. Liberated, mostly by circumstance and sometimes by desire, from male pressure to "make a mark in the world" and "develop the ego," women have served the art and the people. (9)

Thus the intentions of these women, rather than the strategies their work reveals, form the primary focus of Chinoy and Jenkins's work.

In *Feminist Theatre,* Helene Keyssar offers a useful survey of recent American and British drama by women. She describes these plays as united by the "relentless appearance" of a "strategy of transformation, the theatrical manifestation of metamorphosis of contexts, actions and most crucially, of characters. In contrast to most of the drama of the last two thousand years, feminist drama does not rely on a recognition scene as the pivot of its structure" (xiii). Keyssar, however, makes no attempt to substantiate her assertion of a nearly universal presence of a recognition scene in Western drama. Moreover, plays that hinge on a scene of recognition almost invariably depict a transformation of character as a result of this recognition. The distinction between this type of transformation and that seen in feminist theatre is never clarified, nor is Keyssar consistent in pointing out the "strategy of transformation" in all the plays she discusses. She notes in passing other recurrent tendencies in the plays, such as collaboration in writing and an ensemble style of performance, a concern with breaking "the silence too often characteristic of women's place in drama," and a conviction of the "inseparability of sexuality and gender from politics" (3). These observations, however, are never marshaled into a fully articulated, consistent description of feminist theatre.

If Keyssar tends toward the overly inclusive, Elizabeth Natalle errs in the opposite direction. She concludes in *Feminist Theatre: A Study in Persuasion* that feminist theatre (that is, the work of feminist theatre groups) has been a radical form, by which she means that it defines men as the enemy and advocates separatism for women. She notes but does not attempt to resolve the apparently contradictory fact that these groups have recently turned to "humanistic concerns" with such topics as nuclear war and ecology. I believe that the shift in subject matter observed by Natalle reflects a shift in feminist theory from a narrowly defined political struggle to free women from an oppressive patriarchal society toward a broad, encompassing vision including psychological, cultural, and moral as well as political concerns. In this new feminist vision, the struggle is to free not only women, but also men, children, and the planet itself from the oppressions of sex, race, class, technology, and militarism.

Karen Malpede, in her introduction to *Women in Theatre: Compassion and Hope,* reflects some of these concerns in her description of a women's theatre which she believes has mythic roots in the mysteries of the mother goddess. The altruism that she, like Chinoy and Jenkins, traces historically, she relates to women's experiences of mothering. She describes a "theatre arising from the necessity to care for life" in which "the pull together, towards intimacy, is as complex, and as fraught with terror and impossibility, as is the drive toward dominance" (13).

Sue-Ellen Case and Jill Dolan would describe Malpede's philosophy as radical (Case) or cultural (Dolan) feminism, a philosophy they contrast with material feminism. Material feminism is a term both use as inclusive of all socialist and Marxist forms of feminism. Radical/cultural feminism, as Case and Dolan describe it, does not necessarily define man as the enemy, contrary to Natalle's definition. It does, however premise a "woman's culture, different and separate from the patriarchal culture of men" (Case, 64). This assumption of cultural difference based on biological difference, in their view, makes this form of feminism "essentialist" and ultimately self-defeating. If the oppression of women is based on their biological differences from men, there can be no hope of reform. Theatre expressive of this philosophy tends to emphasize the physical bodies of female performers as a way of reclaiming their subjectivity. Basing her argument on semiotics, Dolan responds that "woman, AS subject of desire or of signification, is unrepresentable" (101).

Both Dolan and Case are also critical of the assumption, based on the experience of consciousness-raising groups in the U.S. in the sixties and seventies, that women's shared experience as women overrides differences in class, race, or political commitment. As a result of this assumption, such differences are often overlooked while a white, middle-class, heterosexual bias tends to prevail. Both Dolan and Case argue for a materialist feminist theatre that contradicts this "universalism."

At the point of specific example, however, Dolan and Case part ways. Dolan believes that the lesbian theatre performed, for instance, at the WOW Café and other lesbian coffeehouses in Manhattan embodies materialist feminist theatre practice. Because "gender is foregrounded as a performed role" in these performances, the actors "break the heterosexual contract that informs representation and the enculturation of gender" (101). Case, however, describes such lesbian/separatist theatres as an expression of woman-identified culture characteristic of radical feminism as she has defined it. She envisages instead a "new poetics" which she describes, again in terms drawn from semiotics, as "a reorganisation of theories of libidinal development and dramaturgical devices . . . creat[ing] a new position for the female desiring subject that would change the way the field of signs is constructed" (128). Such a "feminine morphology" would have contiguity as its organizational device:

> It can be elliptical rather than illustrative, fragmentary rather than whole, ambiguous rather than clear, and interrupted rather than complete. This contiguity exists within the text and at its borders: the feminine form seems to be without a sense of formal closure—in fact, it operates as an anti-closure. . . . Without closure, the sense of beginning, middle and end, or a central focus, it abandons the hierarchical organising—principles of traditional form that served to elide women from discourse. (129)

She also speculates that both realism and tragedy may be unsuited to a "feminine morphology." "Realism, in its focus on the domestic sphere and the family unit, reifies the male as sexual subject and the female as the sexual 'Other'" (124). Tragedy might be seen as "a replication of the male sexual experience . . . composed of foreplay, excitation and ejaculation (catharsis). . . . A female form might embody her sexual mode, aligned with multiple orgasms, with no dramatic focus on ejaculation or necessity to build to a single climax" (129). Case notes that this theory leads back, however, to an "essentialist" viewpoint based on biological difference.

Both Case and Dolan seem eager to make a clear-cut distinction between two "feminisms." While Dolan exclusively privileges "materialist feminism," Case instead grants in her closing pages that "certain gains can be realised from both sides of the issue." It seems to me that there are many more than two sides to this issue. Both feminist philosophy and its appearance in contemporary drama are far more multifarious and complex than this dichotomous approach suggests. When we turn from theatre criticism to the new psychology of women and to feminist literary and political theory, the relative exclusivity of Case's and Dolan's approach becomes clearer.

While Case briefly discusses Nancy Chodorow's work on the psychology of women, Dolan bases her belief that women in representation are confined to the role of object on the work of Lacan, who is in turn based upon Freud. Neither author seems to recognize that Chodorow, with Jean Baker Miller and Carol Gilligan, have begun the ground-breaking process of describing a psychology of women which neither objectifies the role of women nor denigrates their experience as an inferior imitation of the male's. Not surprisingly, the patterns of female psychological development that they describe are found reflected in many of the plays I have focused on here.

Josephine Donovan explains in *Feminist Theory* how women's psychology, based on their experience AND their biology, has resulted in the development of an alternative women's culture and ethic. Because women are still almost universally the primary parents in contemporary Western culture, turning away from the mother is essential to the male maturation process. Men's denial of the female has created patriarchal culture, including war, imperialism, and technological destruction of the environment. Women, raised primarily by women, have not experienced the same pattern of development. In addition, they have experienced political oppression unlike that of men; they have typically been assigned to the domestic, rather than the public, sphere; they have functioned economically in production for use, and they have experienced significant physical events different from men. All these differences in experience have resulted in a women's culture and ethic different from men's. This women's culture is apparent in the plays to be discussed.

But just as women have absorbed many aspects of the patriarchal culture, so men may adopt the feminist ethic Donovan describes as including a respect for the contingent order, for the environmental context, and for the concrete world. The nonimperialistic, life-affirming, holistic stance Donovan describes as feminist is one that both women and men may choose or reject. Similarly, this stance can be found in the work of male as well as female playwrights, as I have attempted to illustrate by the inclusion of a play by David Rabe.

Jean Bethke Elshtain, a feminist political theorist, observes that "a feminist politics that does not allow for the possibility of transformation of men as well as women is deeply nihilistic; it does not truly believe in transformative possibilities nor the ideal of genuine mutuality" (349). She envisions instead

> a future social world in which civility and complexity prevail. Such a world would require spheres bearing their own intrinsic dignity and purpose tied to moral and aesthetic imperatives. . . . A richly complex private sphere requires, in order that it survive, freedom from some all-encompassing public imperative, but in order for it to flourish the public world itself must nurture and sustain a set of ethical imperatives, including a commitment to preserve, protect, and defend human beings in their

> capacities as private persons, and to allow men and
> women alike to partake in the good of the public sphere
> on an equal basis of participatory dignity and equality.
> (351)

This vision of a future society is one that I have found reflected in many of these plays.

Feminist theory, in its infancy only a decade ago, has grown into a richly complex subject that is reflected in our society's drama in equally rich and complex ways. In *Feminist Theory: The Intellectual Tradition,* Donovan outlines six distinct strains of feminist philosophy. The first is "enlightenment liberal feminism," originating with Mary Wollstonecraft's *Vindication of the Rights of Woman* (1792), which built upon the idea "that people have certain inalienable or 'natural' rights upon which governments may not intrude," to assert "that women be considered entitled to the same natural rights as men" (1). This form of feminism, still very much alive today, asserts that men and women are essentially similar, and focuses on women's need for legal and educational equality on that basis. In the second chapter, Donovan describes "cultural feminism" of the nineteenth and early twentieth centuries.

> Instead of focusing on political change, feminists holding
> these ideas look for a broader cultural transformation. . . .
> They also stress the role of the non-rational, the intui-
> tive, and often the collective side of life. Instead of
> emphasizing the similarities between men and women,
> they often stress the differences, ultimately affirming
> that feminine qualities may be a source of personal
> strength and pride and a fount of public regeneration.
> (31)

Nineteenth-century cultural feminists generally assumed that the differences between men and women are biologically determined, and that women should enter politics and government in order to bring their innately pacifist, nurturant perspective to the public sphere. Again, this approach to feminism continues to be widely expressed today. After outlining Marxist, Freudian, existentialist, and radical feminist positions, however, Donovan concludes with a description of a "new cultural feminism" which is political as well. Like Elshtain's "politics of compassion," it is characterized by a broad concern for the lives of women, men, and children across cultural and racial boundaries.

The loose network of contemporary feminist philosophies has inspired a literary criticism similarly characterized by a "playful pluralism, responsive to the possibilities of multiple critical schools and methods, but captive of none" (Kolodny 161). While such a pluralistic approach dominates feminist literary criticism today, attempts have been made, specifically in drama, to winnow out the more politically correct "feminist" from the merely "feminine" or "female" (Curb). Such an effort can only serve to suppress certain voices in favor of others, a distinctly antifeminist undertaking. Elaine Showalter, who first employed the terms "feminine," "female," and "feminist" to describe historically distinct phases of women's writing, points out in her final chapter the dilemma the woman writer faces if she sees such categories as absolute and mutually exclusive:

> The radical demand that would yoke women writers to feminist revolution and deny them the freedom to explore new subjects would obviously not provide a healthy direction for the female tradition to take. But the denigration of female experience, the insistence that women deal with "the real business of the world," is also destructive. (318)

Showalter posits instead that "if contact with a female tradition and a female culture is a center; if women take strength in their independence to act in the world, then Shakespeare's sister, whose coming Woolf asked us to await in patience and humility, may appear at last" (319). In this spirit, I outline some prominent themes, strategies, and values of contemporary feminist thought, in order to elucidate some recent feminist drama. In each of the chapters that follow, one of these themes will highlight a detailed analysis of one, two, or three contemporary plays. Yet all these themes are interwoven in all the plays discussed, as I will attempt to show.

Telling Women's Stories

First and most obviously, every field of women's studies, every feminist action is devoted to the recognition and restoration of women who have been silenced and forgotten by the patriarchy. Gerda Lerner, in *The Creation of Patriarchy,* traces women's absence from written history back to history's earliest appearance in ancient Mesopotamia. Because of this exclusion, not from life itself but from what has been heard, recognized, and recorded by the larger society, women have always been regarded as marginal. In a significant analogy, Lerner compares recorded history to a play, in which both men and women

> act out their assigned roles. . . . Neither of them "contributes" more or less to the whole; neither is marginal or dispensable. But the stage set is conceived, painted, defined by men. Men have written the play, have directed the show, interpreted the meaning of the action. . . . Men punish, by ridicule, exclusion, or ostracism, any woman who assumes the right to interpret her own role or—worst of all sins—the right to rewrite the script. (12-13)

To combat this exclusion from the metaphorical (as well as the literal) scripts of society, feminist scholars in every discipline have devoted themselves to the recovery of women's voices.

Annette Kolodny, in "Dancing Through the Minefield," defines the return to circulation of lost works by women as the first task of the feminist literary critic. Carol Christ's *Diving*

Deep and Surfacing: Women Writers on Spiritual Quest begins
with the words:

> Women's stories have not been told. And without stories
> there is no articulation of experience. Without stories a
> woman is lost when she comes to make the important
> decisions of her life. . . . Without stories she is alienated
> from those deeper experiences of self and world that
> have been called spiritual or religious. She is closed in
> silence. The expression of women's spiritual quest is
> integrally related to the telling of women's stories. (1)

Black and lesbian feminists have insisted that they, even
more "invisible" to history than white, middle-class, or
heterosexual women and too often ignored even by these
"sisters," must equally be recognized and heard. Alice Walker
writes, "It is, apparently, inconvenient, if not downright mind
straining, for white women scholars to think of Black women
as women, perhaps because 'woman' (like 'man' among white
males) is a name they are claiming for themselves, and themselves alone" (44). Barbara Smith writes, in "Toward a Black
Feminist Criticism':

> I do not know where to begin. Long before I tried to
> write this I realized that I was attempting something
> unprecedented, something dangerous merely by writing
> about Black women writers from a feminist perspective
> and about Black lesbian writers from any perspective at
> all. These things have not been done. . . . All segments of
> the literary world—whether establishment, progressive,
> Black, female, or lesbian—do not know, or at least act as
> if they do not know, that Black women writers and Black
> lesbian writers exist. (157)

A feminist drama, then, is first of all one that gives voice to
forgotten women.

Thus, when Burke's heroic agent becomes a woman—and
not a young, white, aristocratic woman but a bag lady, a woman
of color, a lesbian or a middle-aged housewife—a new

perception of the world is revealed to the audience. Simply by moving to center stage those who traditionally have been minor characters or offstage altogether, a feminist drama teaches the audience, glorifying the women patriarchal society has defined as marginal. Drama, born of ritual, continues to fulfill ritual functions in contemporary society. "Myth and ritual embody a society's understanding of the universe, for they are attempts to define the human situation and its relationship to the world." Ritual also functions to teach, to influence or control events, and to glorify as well as to give pleasure (Brockett 4). Furthermore, because a play tells its story through dialogue spoken by living performers, these characters are portrayed, not in the abstract language of the patriarchy, but in their own spoken language and in dialogue with one another.

Carol Christ describes a "new women's literature," including drama as well as poetry and novels, that reflects recurrent patterns of woman's social and spiritual quest. The pattern of spiritual quest, on which she focuses, has three parts. First is an experience of nothingness, characterized by self-hatred and victimization. While this is related to the male's experience of ego-less-ness, it is unlike a man's typical experience in that it is imposed from without by the patriarchal society. The second step is an experience of awakening, related to the conversion experience in traditional religions. In women's literature, as Christ describes it, this awakening occurs through a mystical identification with nature or with the community of women. Third is a new naming of self and reality, reflecting a spiritual and psychological wholeness and rejecting the dualisms of self/world, body/soul, and nature/spirit. This pattern, Christ notes, need not occur in linear fashion; it can recur in a spiral pattern instead.

The spiraling plot pattern, a clear-cut contrast with the linear pattern of the dominant culture described by Burke, has been noted by a number of feminist literary theorists. Elizabeth Abel sees two recurrent narrative structures in what she calls "fictions of female development." The first traces "development from childhood conflicts to (frequently imperfect) adult resolutions that provide some closure to the heroine's apprenticeship" (11). Although essentially chronological, the narrative often includes periodic returns to the past resulting in a spiraling progression. This spiral may show an evolutionary progress, or it may spiral downward to death. The second pattern, "the awakening," depicts a woman whose "development is delayed by inadequate education until adulthood, when it blossoms momentarily, then dissolves" (12).

Abel notes that fictions of female development "may revise the conception of protagonist as well. Women characters, more psychologically embedded in relationships, sometimes share the formative voyage with friends, sisters, or mothers, who assume equal status as protagonists" (12). Similarly, Rachel Blau DuPlessis traces narrative quest patterns in the writings of twentieth-century women in which the protagonist

> is a representative of a striving community, breaking with individualism in her rupture from gender-based ends. . . . In the distinctive narrative strategy of the multiple individual, the female hero fuses with a complex and contradictory group; her power is articulated in and continued through a community that is formed in direct answer to the claims of love and romance. (142)

This tendency to resist what DuPlessis calls "the ending in death and . . . the ending in marriage [as] obligatory goals for the female protagonist" (142) has been noted by others as well. Regina Barreca writes:

> For women writers, recognition replaces resolution. Resolution of tensions, like unity or integration, should not be considered viable definitions . . . for women writers because they are too reductive to deal with the non-closed nature of women's writings.

Kathryn Allen Rabuzzi carries women's resistance to traditional story structures to the greatest extreme, suggesting that

the typical domestic life of women, represented mythological-
ly by Hestia/Vesta (a goddess about whom there are no
stories), is simply plotless. Rabuzzi does not regard the plotless
life, however, as meaningless. Instead, she defines the boredom of domestic life as related to the mystical: "Whereas
story, as Aristotle defined it, was made to human measure, the
Mystical and the Boring extend beyond us . . . into the
emptiness of space itself." In contemporary absurdism, she
believes, "women's traditional mode of experiencing life has
finally been given shape artistically. Whether women artists
choose to remain in this mode or not is another issue" (191-
192). It is important to note that, like all the critics cited here,
Rabuzzi is writing description rather than prescription. Her
expectation is that, as fewer women lead a strictly domestic
life, women, including women artists, will experience life
differently and will write out of their new experiences. She is
unwilling, however, to dismiss the traditional female experience as without spiritual value.

While each of these critics examines different specific
works and draws her own conclusions, certain general observations recur. Female writers, they suggest, tend to employ
narrative structures characterized by circular or spiraling patterns, involving a communal protagonist, employing comic
devices of irony and festive license, but resisting the traditionally romantic resolution or, indeed, any clear-cut resolution.

In *The Stick Wife,* by Darrah Cloud, a silenced working-
class housewife is presented with a moral dilemma when she
discovers that it was her husband who bombed a black church,
killing four children. Chapter Two examines this protagonist's
confrontation of her previous complicitous silence and her
eventual coming to speech. Her women friends, as frightened
and willfully ignorant as she has been, nevertheless support
her in the risky choice she makes. The protagonist, then,
becomes a representative of the female community. When she
is threatened by her husband's male accomplices, her women
friends leave their husbands to form a temporary "women's
camp," which is armed with the husbands' guns against the

husbands themselves. Although this brief period of "license" is followed by the return of the protagonist's husband and the breaking up of the women's camp, there is a suggestion of personal, social, and political progress in *The Stick Wife*'s deliberately ambiguous, open ending. At the same time, the final scene closely echoes the opening, resulting in a spiraling, rather than either a linear or a circular, narrative structure.

The Stick Wife does feature the single, heroic protagonist of Burke's paradigm. But as in all the plays by women considered here, she struggles for an autonomy that is neither isolated from nor at odds with her community of friends. Rather, as in many of these plays, the community is both a continual responsibility and a constant source of strength.

Women in Communities

Women's immersion in community has both a political and a psychological base. Politically, the second wave of feminism was founded on that form of community known as the consciousness-raising group. Phyllis Hartsock claims that "the PRACTICE of small-group consciousness raising, with its stress on examining and understanding experience and on connecting personal experience to the structures that define our lives, is the clearest example of the method basic to feminism" (quoted in Donovan, 85). Although the c-r group is a practice borrowed from Marxist theory, Donovan notes that feminists do not employ consciousness-raising as Marxists do, as a basis for ideological construction by a party elite. Rather, she asserts, quoting Gloria Steinem, "feminist theory has focused on 'the integrity of the process of change as part of the change itself. . . . In other words, the end cannot fully justify the means. To a surprising extent, the end IS the means" (87).

Radical feminist theatre groups of the late sixties and seventies often emerged as an expression of consciousness-raising groups, or modeled their theatre companies on the c-r group process. In both Great Britain and the United States, the sixties had been a time of radical experimentation in the theatre. Both male and female playwrights (among them Shelagh Delaney and Ann Jellicoe in Britain, Megan Terry and Maria Irene Fornes in the U.S.) broke with the structure and conventions of realism to create plays that often were critical of the Establishment and didactic in intention. These plays attempted in Brechtian style to break down the barrier between audience and performers, sometimes by ensemble performances in which the same actor played several roles (Keyssar, 22-52).

This radical style of theatre married with the politics and structure of the feminist consciousness-raising group to produce the feminist theatre group in Great Britain in the late sixties, and a few years later in the United States. Typically a nonprofessional, shoestring operation, the feminist theatre group presented highly didactic pieces, often created by the group. Some groups performed only for women, while others saw consciousness-raising in the larger community as a goal. Most employed only female performers, though a few included male actors as needed. Often a performance was comprised of a series of sketches or monologues rather than following one protagonist through an extended plot as in traditional Western drama (Natalle; Brown, 96-113).

Undoubtedly, these performances have influenced the work of individual playwrights of the late seventies and the eighties in creating plays with a group protagonist. Honor Moore calls these "choral plays":

> Approaching women's experience through the strategy of telling the story of an individual woman's struggle for autonomy results in what I call "the autonomous woman play," while choosing the strategy of dramatizing a situation which involves a group of women (or women and men) results in "the choral play.". . . The choral plays show us women together, women seeking integration by attempting community, much as women did in consciousness-raising groups. (186-187)

For women of color, doubly oppressed by racial and sexual discrimination, community has been a source both of comfort and of conflict. As Gerda Lerner notes in *Black Women in White America,* "Black women . . . have been nearly unanimous in their insistence that . . . their liberation depends on the liberation of the race and the improvement of the life of the black community" (xxv). Yet within the black community, their struggle against sexism continues. Two plays that depict black women in community will be examined in Chapter Three: *For Colored Girls Who Have Considered Suicide When the Rainbow Is Enuf* by Ntozake Shange, and Kathleen Collins's play, The *Brothers.*

Moore also describes plays in which a group of women portray a single protagonist. "The protagonist is divided into several selves, each of whom expresses different versions of the woman in question" (187). By its implication of a diffused ego, such a strategy evokes the work of Jean Baker Miller and Nancy Chodorow in female psychology and of Carol Gilligan in female moral development.

Female Moral and Psychological Development

Jean Baker Miller believes that referring to "the ego, the 'I' of psychoanalysis, may not be at all appropriate when talking about women. Women have different organizing principles around which their psyches are structured. One of these principles is that they exist to serve other people's needs" (62). In *The Reproduction of Mothering,* Nancy Chodorow says, "The basic feminine sense of self is connected to the world, the basic masculine sense of self is separate" (169). She attributes this difference to the fact that women, almost universally, are the primary parents in our society. "Mothers tend to experience their daughters as more like, and continuous with, themselves. Correspondingly, girls tend to remain part of the dyadic primary mother-child relationship itself. . . . From very early, then . . . girls come to experience themselves as less differentiated than boys, as more continuous with and related to the external object-world" (166-167).

Building on Chodorow's work, Carol Gilligan has described a distinctly female pattern of moral development. The moral development of men, until recently considered the norm, tends to progress from a concern for rules and rights to a more mature sense of responsibility and concern for others. But because of the sense of connection with the world that Chodorow describes, "women not only define themselves [initially] in a context of human relationship but also judge themselves in terms of their ability to care" (Gilligan, 17). For women, maturity comes with "questioning the stoicism of self-denial and replacing the illusion of innocence with an awareness of choice. . . . Then the notion of care expands from the paralyzing injunction not to hurt others to an injunction to act responsively toward self and others and thus to sustain connection" (149).

In Chapter Four, two plays by Marsha Norman will be considered, both demonstrating distinctly female patterns of moral and psychological development. In *Getting Out,* the protagonist is represented by two actresses, one portraying the character's present self, devoted to gaining custody of her son by leading a life of denial, and one portraying her past self, a willful juvenile delinquent struggling for survival. In *'Night, Mother,* the characters are mother and daughter, and the play's central issue is the merging and separation Chodorow describes, as the daughter tries to prepare her mother to accept the daughter's decision to commit suicide.

A New Feminist Ethic

Because women have shared the experience of political oppression, of assignment to the domestic sphere, of production for use rather than for exchange, and of significant physical events that differ from men's, women have formed a particular consciousness and a particular ethic. This ethic, as described by Donovan, is

> based on a fundamental respect for the contingent order,
> for the environmental context, for the concrete, every-
> day world. Women more than men appear to be willing
> to adopt a passive mode of accepting the diversity of
> environmental "voices" and the validity of their realities.
> Women appear less willing to wrench that context apart
> or to impose upon it alien abstractions or to use imple-
> ments that subdue it intellectually or physically. Such an
> epistemology provides the basis for an ethic that is non-
> imperialistic, that is life-affirming, and that reverences
> the concrete details of life. (173)

This ethic, while created by women's experience, need not
be limited to women in application. Indeed, as Elshtain maintains, the radical feminist characterization of men as onto-
logical oppressors who are incapable of change and of wom-
en as eternal victims is simply a mirror image of the patriarchal world view. Elshtain, with many others, calls for an
extension of woman's private moral sense into the public
sphere:

> If it is the case that women have a distinct moral lan-
> guage, as Carol Gilligan has argued, one which em-
> phasizes concern for others, responsibility, care and
> obligation, hence a moral language profoundly at odds
> with formal, abstract models of morality defined in terms
> of absolute principles, then we must take care to pre-
> serve the sphere that makes such a morality of responsi-
> bility possible and extend its imperatives to men as well.
> (335)

This major shift in feminist thought is reflected in two plays
by David Rabe examined in Chapter Five, *In the Boom Boom
Room* (1973) and *Hurlyburly* (1985). *In the Boom Boom Room*
sympathetically portrays a go-go dancer's doomed attempt at
self-expression in the patriarchal underworld of Philadel-
phia's "combat zone." The play is a male writer's portrayal of
woman's struggle for personal autonomy. As such, it offers an
instructive comparison with the work of female playwrights

addressing similarly feminist themes. *Hurlyburly* revolves around a group of morally bankrupt men on the fringes of the Los Angeles film community. Its resolution comes with the male protagonist's recognition of wisdom in the words of an exploited teenage girl. Reflecting the impact of feminism on the lives of men, *Hurlyburly* also relates feminism to broad societal concerns, making it a complex and moving expression of a contemporary feminist ethic presented from a male perspective.

Societal Transformation

Recent feminist theory has shifted in emphasis from the individual's struggle for autonomy to the need for societal transformation. Bell Hooks asserts that

> neither a feminism that focuses on woman as an autonomous human being worthy of personal freedom nor one that focuses on the attainment of equality of opportunity with men can rid society of sexism and male domination. Feminism is a struggle to end sexist oppression. Therefore, it is necessarily a struggle to eradicate the ideology of domination that permeates Western culture on various levels as well as a commitment to reorganizing society so that the self-development of people can take precedence over imperialism, economic expansion, and material desires. (24)

Barbara Ehrenreich, in the fifteenth anniversary issue of *Ms.* Magazine, notes a possible reason for this shift in emphasis. She writes that the middle-class feminist movement, long the leadership, "has been showing disturbing signs of lethargy," perhaps because of its relative success in at least one area: the professions have largely opened their doors to women. "In 1970, fewer than 8 percent of the nation's physicians were female; today, 14.6 percent are female and approximately 30 percent of our medical students are women, and the gains are of the same magnitude in law and business" (168). Ehrenreich bemoans the resultant attitude on the part of young middle- and upper-class women, "that, whatever indignities women may have suffered in the remote past (for example, 1970), the way is now clear for any woman of spirit to rise straight to the top of whatever fascinating, lucrative profession she chooses" (168). In contrast, Ehrenreich notes,

> feminist consciousness appears to rise as one descends the socioeconomic scale. Fifty-five percent of women with family incomes of over $40,000 a year are self-identified feminists, compared to 57 percent of women with family incomes of under $20,000 a year. . . . Non-white women were the most feminist of all [in the 1987 Gallup Poll] with 64 percent declaring themselves feminist. (216)

"What the statistics seem to be saying," Ehrenreich concludes, "is that the women who are most favorably disposed to feminism today are the ones who have gained the least from the movement so far, and hence have the most to gain from the struggle."

Caryl Churchill's play, *Top Girls,* analyzed in Chapter Six, sharply delineates the clash created by this distinction between personal and political forms of feminism. *Top Girls* is introduced by a fantasy scene in which remarkable women from all periods of history meet at a dinner party to celebrate the promotion of Marlene, a woman executive. The remainder of the play, set in the present day, presents in Marlene's family and fellow workers the silencing, the isolation, and the destructive imitations of male psychology and morality that follow from a purely personal quest for autonomy.

Despite the bleakness of its vision, *Top Girls* is, like many of the works examined here, a very funny play. Three plays that, despite the seriousness of their intent, find comic or even romantic expression, form the subject of Chapter Seven.

Comedy and Romance

In my first attempt to define feminist drama, I found Burke's
pentad an awkward tool, perhaps because it is based on an
essentially tragic model. Burke's solitary agent, like every
tragic hero from Oedipus onward, struggles in a state of
elevated isolation and high seriousness against his implacable
fate. While the history of drama reveals a handful of tragic
heroines (invariably male creations), the real lives of women
have seldom provided the elevated status, the isolation, or the
ability to take one's self and one's fate as seriously as a tragic
hero must do.

On the other hand, and flying in the face of a long line of
female writers and performers of comedy, critics have for
centuries stoutly maintained that women "have no sense of
humor." Linda Martin and Kerry Segrave observe in their
introduction to *Women in Comedy:*

> Virtually none of the women in this book started out
> with the idea of being a comic. . . . It was considered
> unladylike for women to do physical humor, and unfemi-
> nine for them to do hard-edged verbal satire, because of
> its aggressive qualities.

Regina Barreca quotes J. B. Priestley and Reginald Blyth, who
condemn women writers in much the same terms: "The truth
is . . . that women have not only no humor in themselves but
are the cause of the extinction of it in others" (Blyth, quoted in
Barreca, 4).

As in other realms of feminist theory, however, new ground
is being broken in the field of women's comedy. Barreca calls
comedy "a way women writers can reflect the absurdity of the
dominant ideology while undermining the very basis for its
discourse" (19). Gagnier, Brownstein, and Spacks describe in
Barreca's anthology how female writers of prose from Austen
to Woolf have used wit and irony to accomplish such an
undermining of patriarchy.

Barreca goes on to suggest:

> Certainly recent feminist criticism has accepted the chal-
> lenge of providing new patterns and strategies to charac-
> terize women's narrative discourse. There is no reason
> comedy and humor should be excluded from this revi-
> sionist criticism. The interpretive applications for come-
> dy written by women have been narrowed by the inherit-
> ed critical structures which do not provide for the
> particularly insurgent strategies used by women writers.
> To explain further: without subverting the authority of
> her own writing by breaking down convention complete-
> ly, the woman comic writer displays a different code of
> subversive thematics than her male counterpart. (9)

In particular, comic conventions of romance and the happy
ending have been put to unconventional ends, parodied, or
disregarded altogether by women writers.

Judy Little, in an examination of the comic writing of
Virginia Woolf and Muriel Spark, describes the imagery of
women's comedy as "usually that of festive license or of an
important passage in life. Further, such imagery—imagery of
revolt and inversion—is ordinarily not resolved in the fiction
of these authors" (1). Unlike the traditional comedy described
by Northrop Frye, in which the hero is reintegrated into a
restored society, often through marriage, here the ending is
left open.

Little maintains further that women writers seldom adopt a
traditional quest pattern (such as Burke describes) with its
clear-cut sense of resolution, because the underlying myth is
"allowed" only to the highly individualized, invariably male
protagonist. "Even when the imagery suggests myth, the
archetypal imagery is in the first place suggestive of a female
iconography, not a male one; and secondly, the mythic imagery is treated ironically" (187).

Jane Wagner's *The Search for Signs of Intelligent Life in the
Universe,* Jane Chambers's *Last Summer in Bluefish Cove,* and
Holly Hughes's *The Well of Horniness* provide a broad spec-

trum of contemporary feminist comedy. *The Search,* a one-woman vehicle for Lily Tomlin, presents a kaleidoscopic array of (mostly female) protagonists, and a style of humor clearly designed to urge reexamination of societal conventions. While romance is simply dismissed in *The Search,* it is inverted and mocked in *The Well,* a lesbian parody of the conventions of mystery thrillers, soap operas, and pornographic movies. *Last Summer* presents lesbian subjects in a realistic style, offering a gently humorous, bittersweet romance.

Entering the Mainstream

Drama, more than any other literary form, is a public act, complete only when it is performed before an audience. It may reinforce the audience's attitudes, or it may challenge, provoke, or offend them. But it will not survive as a public act if it does not speak somehow to its audience. It is, therefore, of particular interest when a viewpoint such as feminism, once seen as extreme, makes its way into mainstream, commercial theatre. Feminist dramas may and often do vie with plays expressive of other, sometimes hostile, viewpoints. I believe that the success of these plays nevertheless represents an important shift in public consciousness. For this reason, all the plays considered at length here are commercially successful works that have received professional productions in the United States. All but *The Stick Wife* have been published, most as individual volumes. The emergence of such a body of commercial feminist drama on the American stage in the last ten years is not to be lightly dismissed. These plays represent one of the most hopeful indications that the feminist awareness of the sixties and seventies has, in a broader form, entered the mainstream of American consciousness.

As Patti Gillespie notes in explaining the appropriateness of drama as a form of feminist rhetoric, "As a symbol, theatre says more than its literal meaning and means more than a single thing. Public address and debate are more nearly confined to the presentation of systematic arguments. Theatre has no such obligation: it can present a version of 'reality' in all its complexity and contradiction" (281-282). What follows is a discussion of some of the most exciting feminist versions, visions, and revisions of reality in U.S. theatre today.

2 • *The Stick Wife*

The Stick Wife, by Darrah Cloud, began in 1983 with the playwright's encounter of a *New York Times* report on the FBI investigation into the 1963 bombing of a Birmingham, Alabama, church. "There was one paragraph about the wives of these men, who'd run a kind of covert operation, informing on their husbands," Cloud recalled in a newspaper interview. "I would never have written a play about the bombing; I'm just not into documentaries. But when I read about the women, how they lived with these men—and at the same time were talking with the FBI. . . . How could you live with somebody and hate what they do?" (Cloud, "The Tough Life"). The play that resulted from Cloud's effort to answer that question is by no means documentary; rather, it is a surreal, darkly humorous rendering of one woman's progress from a victimized silence into the speech of moral witness. Her action threatens her friends, her sanity, and her life itself, but her oppressive relationship with her husband and her own sense of self-worth are subtly yet profoundly transformed.

The play, which had its premiere at the Los Angeles Theatre Center in 1987, received mixed reviews in the Los Angeles press. Reviewers prepared to see a play on civil rights were disappointed by "Cloud's insistence on intertwining sexism and racism" (Fried). A production at the Hartford Stage Company later that year was more positively received, with

Excerpts from *The Stick Wife,* by Darrah Cloud, reprinted by permission of the author.

praise for the designs, the direction (by Roberta Levitow, who directed the premiere as well) and the acting, especially Lois Smith's in the leading role. Mel Gussow, writing for the *New York Times,* however, still insisted that, "the effort to equate racism and sexism is not proven. The husband's abuse of his wife is simply not equal to his murder of innocent black children. But once Ms. Cloud fixes her images, it is difficult to avert our attention."

Gussow's implication that racism and sexism are simplistically equated does an injustice to the complexity of the play. The humor surrounding the wives' duplicitous behavior with their husbands does not compare but contrasts with the women's horrified response to the death of four black children in the bombing. Gussow more closely approaches the real point of the play in his praise for *The Stick Wife*'s attention to these silenced, invisible women.

The Stick Wife, set in the summer of 1963 in Birmingham, takes place in the "shoddy backyard" of Ed and Jessie Bliss. The stage directions note "a maze of clotheslines" and the "junk of marriage" lying around. Scene 1 is a laconic exchange between Ed, who has come into the backyard to get work clothes off the line, and his wife Jessie, who attempts unsuccessfully to find out where Ed is going on a Sunday morning and when he will return. She offers to make apple pancakes, threatens to follow him or to leave him while he's out, and finally pleads, "Don't go! Don't go!" Ed responds, "You knew where I was goin' you wouldn't say that," and when she continues to plead, concludes, "See there? You don't know nothin'" (4). Jessie's isolation, her ignorance, and her helpless dependence on Ed are strikingly established.

That afternoon, Jessie is hanging white sheets on the clothesline, ignoring the ringing phone, and fantasizing that she is a movie star. Her neighbor Marguerite appears, saying, "I could hear you over here not answerin' the phone!" and when Jessie tries to escape into the house, pleads, "Please don't go! . . . You hear the news?" (5). Jessie and Marguerite struggle, Jessie to avoid hearing "the news," Marguerite to share her awful knowledge: "Somebody bombed a colored church. [JESSIE pulls her dress up over her head.] I'm sorry! I'm sorry! I just couldn't hold it in!" (7). The women's horror stems only partly from the sacrilege of such an act. Despite their best efforts to ignore the truth, they are already half-conscious that their husbands—through their "Club"—are responsible for the bombing. Marguerite suggests they pray that "nobody got hurt in that exploded church," and adds to her prayer, "There's still time to take it back, Lord. We haven't heard it on the news yet" (14). When Ed returns in muddy work clothes with a large amount of cash, Jessie tells him his clothes cannot be cleaned; what they have on them is "not just dirt" (19).

Big Albert arrives with his wife, Betty, looking for Ed, who has gone out again to see the effect of the bombing on the town. Betty manages to let Jessie know covertly that four children were killed in the bombing. Jessie is so shaken by this news that Big Albert wonders if she is sick. Jessie responds, "I depend so on the weather as to how I feel. . . . What's it doin' up there today? I can't think." "I'll tell you what to think," Big Albert says, and Jessie responds, "I wish someone would" (27). When everyone has gone, Jessie returns to her laundry and her fantasies: "This . . . is my lovely estate . . . I . . . decorated it . . . in white. . . . I clean from top to bottom every day. . . . It's how I pray" (28).

Scene 3 on Monday morning finds Jessie once again hanging out wash. Marguerite returns for another visit, followed by Betty, who struggles vainly to speak to Jessie alone. Finally she scribbles on a card and tells Jessie, "Here's that recipe I promised." Jessie reads the card and responds, shocked, "Ed?" (41). Obviously, the card names Ed as the man responsible for the church bombing, but Betty refuses to share the secret with Marguerite. Instead she tells her it is a secret recipe for white bread, and goes on to spin a hilarious story to cover Jessie's weeping:

> That recipe come across the ocean with my Great-great-grandmother! She brought it from the deserts of France where the women gathered once a year in the caves and took off alla their clothes and danced together till the Virgin Mary appeared and talked to them in a tongue they'd never heard before but still understood. . . . Girls, she said, don't never go inta politics. Politics is just a buncha rules we make up so's we don't hafta face ourselves and change. Girls, she said, they's a whole 'nother world in the world. A whole 'nother world! Then she blew her nose in a maple leaf even though there weren't no maples in France and said, she weren't no virgin! . . . She just didn't want kids! . . . [They roll and scream with laughter.] (42)

The women's moment of community is interrupted by Big Albert, who has come to take Betty home. He tells Jessie that Ed has been arrested for the church bombing, but reassures her, "That's OK, honey. Half the p'lice force belongs to the Club. Whoever told on Ed, we gonna shut him up" (47). He warns her to stay at home, and closes the act with a kind of combined reassurance and threat: "We gonna be watchin' out for you. . . . You do anythin' against Ed, anythin', we gonna come after you" (48b).

Act 2, in November of the same year, opens again on Jessie's yard. The clotheslines are now decked with red dresses, and the white sheets are piled on the ground as a bed for Jessie. As the scene begins, she rises from the sheets "like a phoenix," eats something off the ground, and finally goes to the laundry pole, "stretches against it luxuriously; turns and then straddles the pole, moves against it sensuously" as Marguerite enters, screaming, "Get in your house!" Their dialogue reveals that Jessie, still without Ed, now lives entirely in the backyard. Jessie tells Marguerite her house is haunted by ghosts which she later describes as "all over Birmingham

. . . white ghost people . . . can't find the bodies they come from" (55).

Marguerite has come to warn Jessie that the men are coming to "shut her up." Jessie pleads that she doesn't remember how to entertain, and asks Marguerite to tell them to "come another time. . . . Tell 'em I got a headache!" (53). Marguerite runs off, and Tom and Big Albert enter wearing red war paint and "either hunting or camouflage army gear" (55). Jessie recognizes them at once in their disguises, but they claim, "That ain't me!" The men want to know why Jessie has not visited her husband in jail; she claims her car wouldn't start. The men conclude that Jessie has "forgot howta act," and warn her that "rapists and robbers" will "slit your throat and rip your voice-box out and leave it wrigglin' in the dirt like a newborn" (62-63). As they move in to attack her, Jessie screams, and Betty and Marguerite run on from the alley. In mock surprise, they call out their husbands' names, and ask them, "You cheatin' on us?" (64). Tom flies into a rage against Marguerite, but Albert stops him from attacking her, and tells the women to go into the house and bring Tom something to drink.

When the men are left alone, Tom confesses he cannot control his anger: "I get powers! Special powers! . . . Don't know if they come from God or Space. When I go back to bein' myself, I got nothin' . . . I'm nothin'" (66). Marguerite and Betty return with water and cookies, and Tom and Big Albert begin to rage at them again, insisting that men are engaged in an "undeclared war" and that the women are trying to stop them. As they close in on their wives, Jessie appears with a gun and stops them. With the words, "NOBODY UNDER-STANDS YOU!" she drives them off "reeling with rage" (71-72).

Jessie had found a collection of rifles Ed was keeping for men in the Club, and now issues the women the guns with their husbands' names on them. Marguerite wants to go home: "I'm nothin' without my man! . . . I wanta stay home! . . . I wanta bake and clean and sing and talk to God all day! Go places at night! Places I can't go without a man!" (74). Betty and Marguerite try to warn her that Tom will not take her back, but when she insists, Jessie says, "We can't keep her here against herself" (75). Marguerite goes home, but comes back almost immediately, having discovered that she is locked out. Jessie insists that they stay outside all night, since "a house can get blown up" (77). The women improvise a fort in the backyard, and bring the television out with an extension cord since Betty cannot sleep without it. The scene ends with Jessie taking the first watch. She returns to her fantasies: "I gave up Hollywood . . . I'm one of the few who ever got out. . . . I got so sick . . . of all those jackasses tellin' me how to act" (80).

Marguerite and Betty wake up the next afternoon to find Jessie glued to the television: John F. Kennedy has just been shot. The women react with grief and fear: "Who's gonna take care of us?" (83). Betty and Marguerite try to reassure Jessie that Ed will be back, but she insists he will not. Finally she confesses, "I'm the one turned him in!" (85). The other women react immediately by telling her "Shut up!" but she says she is "tired of shuttin' up! . . . That's who I am!" (85). Breaking glass is heard inside, and the women take up their guns, wondering, "Who they gonna be this time?" (88). Tom and Albert appear in street clothes, speaking civilly, and Marguerite runs to Tom to kiss him, "as if saved" (88). Ed appears next, and Jessie turns her gun on him.

The other couples leave the two at gunpoint, telling one another that Jessie "just doesn't believe" her husband is really back. Left alone, Ed takes the gun from Jessie and begins a banal conversation about the men he saw in prison. He implies that he was released through pressure from other Club members. As he starts to leave again, Jessie says with "renewed strength," "Where ya goin'? Ed? [He halts; looks at her.] Where you goin'?" The play ends on this somewhat ambiguous note. While Jessie has failed to see Ed punished, Ed has returned to her, willing to overlook the possibility that it was she who turned him in. She has not received an answer to her question, "Where you goin'?" by the play's end, but she is now able at least to stop Ed and gain his attention.

Darrah Cloud has said:

> I wrote *The Stick Wife* because I had a theory about
> sexism and racism: that it comes from the same place
> within ourselves. I wanted to find out where that place
> was; and what else came out of it besides hate for those
> we perceive as weaker than us, whom we demand be
> weaker so that we might take out our hate of weakness on
> the definitive, widely-accepted weak, thereby punish-
> ing the weakness in ourselves. (Cloud, "From the
> Playwright")

The lower-class white southern neighborhood in which the
play takes place is a crucible of racial and class tensions. Ed
complains that wealthy whites are "over the mountain in they
livin' rooms. Talkin 'bout rights at cocktail parties. . . . No
colored movin' into their neighborhoods. Movin' into ours.
We white as them. . . . Come we don't get nothin' for it?"
Instead of receiving privileged treatment, Ed feels he is
ignored: "People don't even know me are thinkin' I'm nothin'
right now" (22). Big Albert, attempting to persuade Jessie that
he is not himself, describes Big Albert as "that chump, that
loser, that poor white trash" (56). As Cloud suggests, it is the
weakness and the invisibility of the poor whites that drives the
men to acts of violence.

The women are by no means immune to class issues. Jessie,
fantasizing that she knows the Kennedys, describes them as
"just poor white trash that made it. . . . Why do you want to
know about them? Why don't you want to know about me?"
(44). Yet they are entirely outside the men's "undeclared war"
on blacks, guilty only of deliberate ignorance of the men's
behavior. Instead, their existence centers on their homes,
their children and their women friends, on the female subculture they have created within the larger community.

Rabuzzi notes in *The Sacred and The Feminine* that "some
aspects of feminine culture are so separate and hidden that
they scarcely penetrate the dominant culture even tacitly"
(21). So it is with Jessie, Marguerite, and Betty, to whom the
emerging Vietnam conflict is just an example of men "hellin'
around as usual. . . . Gettin' away from the wives" (40). Their

own lives revolve around the endless repetition of chores and backyard chats, which the play ultimately reveals as "a kind of gnosis, a special knowledge, even a heresy, with explicit rites and rituals of its own" (Rabuzzi, 21). Jessie's incessant laundering of sheets is clearly the ritual purification described by Rabuzzi, serving "to exorcise, for the woman washing . . . her own spiritual deformities" (115). When she has spoken against Ed, her sin is expunged and so her washing ceases.

Marguerite, in constantly seeking out Jessie's company, enacts the homecoming ritual of the coffee klatch. Since a homebound woman cannot experience the return to her own house as a homecoming, Rabuzzi speculates that she may turn to visits in the home of women friends:

> Though the coffee klatch phenomenon does, perhaps, seem like a luxurious "waste" of time to individuals forced into masculine, linear time, to construe it that way is to miss its significance. In one sense, it is both life saving and life giving, helping to alleviate the truly terrible loneliness so characteristic of the traditional homebound feminine existence. (136)

Clearly, Jessie, Betty, and Marguerite form such a "life saving" community for one another. Not only do they literally protect one another at gunpoint from the men, they reinforce each other's survival skills. When Marguerite prepares to leave the women's encampment, Betty advises her:

> Man won't generally go off on you when he's with another woman. But you see a pack a men, you run. You see a man alone, you run again. They not all bad. . . . But . . . they all look alike. . . . You'd have to marry 'em all to find out who they really are! (76)

Further, as Betty's description of her female ancestors' worshiping the Virgin suggests, their community has religious and moral functions as well. When Marguerite suggests to Jessie that they kneel and pray together, she remarks that her instincts are sound; "I just don't listen to 'em" except in the presence of her women friends (14). The men justify the church bombing by defining their situation as "undeclared war." In a patriarchal ethic, killing in time of war is permitted. Among themselves, however, the women confirm their own view: "Them poor little girls! How their Mamas ever gonna live without them?" (31). As Carol Gilligan would suggest is typical, these women make moral judgments in a context of empathic care rather than of principle. Rejecting the rule-oriented ethic of the men, Betty has the Virgin herself declare, "Politics is just a buncha rules we make up so's we don't hafta face ourselves and change" (42).

Jessie is undoubtedly strengthened by this community in the decision to "face herself and change." But she makes her decision alone. Rabuzzi maintains that the "terrible loneliness" of the homebound woman has both a demonic and a sacred aspect. Especially for a woman like Jessie, whose children have grown and gone, housekeeping can be demonic in its triviality and its isolation. Yet the homemaker can move through the surface boredom of her constantly repeated chores to enter into a mystical state of nothingness. Like Marguerite, who wants to "bake and clean and sing and talk to God all day," such a woman can make contact with the divine and with her own deepest self in the monotonous isolation of her home.

Jessie's inner journey can be tracked through her soliloquies, in which she fantasizes herself a movie star. In the first one, she describes having worked with Gary Cooper: "he had a very rare skin disease . . . his skin was like Saran Wrap . . . we starlets were afraid ta kiss him for fear of suffocatin'. . . ." Her condition as the play opens is indeed dangerously close to suffocation by a man—her husband, who will not speak honestly nor listen to her. The scene in which she realizes Ed may have been responsible for the church bombing concludes with a description of her fantasied start in show business: "I was discovered bein' a female at a cash register . . . I married the man who discovered me . . . and now I look back and I wonder, what happened to all those girls I knew who wanted what I got? . . . Why me?" (17). Like the stereotypical starlet discovered working in a drugstore, Jessie was "discovered" by Ed and married him simply because he asked her, taking a completely passive role. Her question, "Why me?" is ironic. As a starlet, she wonders why she was lucky enough to be discovered, but as Jessie, she wonders why she was so unlucky as to be married to the man who has now committed a terrible crime. In act 2, her decision to witness against Ed already made, she describes "giving up" acting. She has abandoned her attempt to play the roles imposed by the patriarchy; now she will be herself.

The Hollywood soliloquies are full of references to her children, whom she says were "taken" from her because of show business. In fact, Ed and Jessie's dialogue in scene 1 has revealed that their children have grown up and left home, and that their whereabouts are unknown to their parents. Ed says they will not come back because Jessie "poisoned 'em against me," implying that it is Ed they are avoiding, yet it is Jessie who mourns their loss. In this first scene of the play, the only defense of her own worth that Jessie can muster is, "I raised two children!" (4). Later, the news that four children died in the church bombing moves Jessie from her former extreme passivity to the extreme moral action of witnessing against her husband. Throughout the play she speculates on what mistake she made in raising them, and finally concludes that she let them watch too much TV, "and they think people were made just to entertain 'em. Me, I'm too real for them to come and see . . . I'm very real" (23).

The playwright suggests that for Jessie, "morality was not the issue. It served as no guide. Poverty and ignorance make morality look like more poverty and ignorance: a losing position. So Jessie's actions aren't moral: they are all about survival, and she would not have survived if she had left her man. She was an accidental heroine" (Cloud, "From the Playwright," 5). Yet Jessie believes that by turning Ed in to the police, she *has* left him. She tells the other women it as though he had died: "He ain't never comin' back!" (84). Nor has she chosen the obvious route to survival by turning him in; it would have been much safer to ignore the whole issue. As Big Albert and Tom point out, she has no money or job experience and in any case, "ain't no jobs" for people of their class and education. Jessie may not have formulated her decision as a moral one, knowing it contradicted the dominant culture, but like a female Huck Finn, she follows her own "gut" sense of right and wrong, what Carol Gilligan calls an "ethic of care."

Gilligan describes a distinctly female pattern of moral development which progresses from (1) an initial focus on self to assure survival to (2) the development of a sense of responsibility for others, manifested through self-sacrifice, to (3) a broad perspective on the interconnection between self and other which dissolves the tension between selfishness and responsibility (73-74). In the course of *The Stick Wife*, Jessie moves from a selfish attempt to ignore the bombing for the sake of her own survival to a sense of responsibility for the dead children, built perhaps on her feeling for her own lost children, which moves her to self-sacrifice by sacrificing her husband, her only support. The unexpected result of this self-sacrifice is, however, a fully realized self. Moved originally by a motherly concern for the murdered black children, Jessie finds she has acted not only on their behalf but on her own, dissolving the tension between selfishness and responsibility.

Jessie's decision to witness against Ed is not revealed to the audience until well into the second act, but the metamorphosis her character has undergone is clear the moment act 2 begins. Her obsessive washing of sheets has ended, to be replaced by a stage hung with bright red dresses. Symbolically, she has abandoned the futile effort to remain innocent of Ed's crime; she embraces instead the red both of violence and of regenerative female blood. No longer a housewife, she has left the house to ghosts, the souls of whites lost to their owners by their racist actions. Her own behavior is uncivilized, openly sexual, apparently "crazy." Yet she tells Marguerite "This is

the real me. . . . You've just never seen me happy before"
(51).

Jessie's happiness results from her decision to speak the
truth. Although her already marginal status in society has now
been lost, making her fair game for any man's violence, she has
abandoned deception and thus has been restored to herself.
As Susan Griffin writes:

> When we speak of deception, we must speak of a self
> destroyed. For the deceiver has two selves. One is a false
> self, manufactured for appearance' sake and set before an
> audience. . . . But the other self, who is the real self, is
> consigned to silence. . . . Thus the deceiver is in danger
> of never remembering that she has a real self. The real
> self continues to experience, to feel, to move through
> life. But in our minds, we destroy her experience and
> thus we destroy ourselves. (202)

Jessie, by breaking her soul-destroying silence, not only
avenges the dead children, not only liberates herself, but
profoundly shakes both the male and the female members
of her community. Big Albert and Tom are so deeply threatened by the mere suspicion of Jessie's witness that they plan a
violent attack on her—and then are frightened off when she
confronts them. Betty and Marguerite are moved to a risky
though still veiled defense of Jessie against their own husbands. In their encampment, all three women find that Jessie's
initial act of speech has empowered them to break with a
lifetime of lies and silences. Marguerite admits, "I am sick to
death of everybody thinkin' I'm stupid!" and Jessie responds,
"They got to, otherwise, they won't talk to you" (78). Marguerite says, "Someday I'm gonna explode and die from all I
held in," and Betty answers, "That's how you get back at them"
(78).

Finally, Ed's relationship to Jessie is profoundly altered by
her speech, as the play's conclusion reveals. As soon as they
are left alone, both Ed and Jessie revert to the banal, monosyl-
labic speech of the first scene. Eventually, they are repeating

the very dialogue with which the play began. Yet their relationship has undergone a metamorphosis. Despite an appearance of circularity, everything has changed. Rabuzzi suggests that the traditional Aristotelian plot structure with its beginning, middle, and end may not be the appropriate form in which to portray the housewife's existence. Instead, "When recognizable temporal progression ceases . . . the lyric mode dominates and we end up with . . . stories in which nothing happens, just as 'nothing happens' in traditional women's mode of being, the waiting mode" (167). While relatively little "happens" in *The Stick Wife,* it cannot be described as entirely in the waiting mode.

Jessie, with the help of her women friends, faces her husband's crime and her own complicity in it. By witnessing against this crime, she enters what Carol Christ would call "the deep," the subconscious realm of madness in her backyard. When the other women join her there, they share for a night her experience of this realm, forming a women's community. The consciousness of all the women is changed in the course of this night, making the conclusion less circular than spiraling. Jessie, in particular, is awakened to the true meaning of her marriage and her life before taking up that subtly transformed marriage and life again.

As in traditional comedy, the women all return unpunished to their husbands in the morning. Yet despite the restored marriages, *The Stick Wife* is deeply antiromantic. While Marguerite, the silliest of the women, tries to mimic romance with her loutish husband, even she finally admits that she needs to be married primarily to survive in the patriarchy. Underlying Jessie's romantic daydreams of movie stardom is an unglamorous longing to be reunited with her children, recognized by her husband, and freed of her intolerable situation. While this play builds on the traditional comic ending, it erects a far different structure there. Though the couples are restored, they show every sign of living together less peacefully than before. The society around them, similarly, is in upheaval at the end of the play. No new and more perfect order has been established. Rather, the play reaches an uneasy, momentary stasis.

One of the recurrent narrative structures described in *The Voyage In* is that of "the awakening." In this pattern, "development is delayed by inadequate education until adulthood, when it blossoms momentarily, then dissolves" (Abel, Hirsch, and Langland, 12). Named for Kate Chopin's short story about a woman whose journey of self-discovery ends in suicide, this pattern suggests that a self-aware woman (at least of the nineteenth and early twentieth century) will be so frustrated by the limitations of her society that she will choose death as "a realistic and paradoxically fulfilling reaction to an impossible contradiction" (28). Although Jessie's circumstances in 1963 are hardly less constraining than those of the last century, she survives her awakening. Indeed, while her accomplishment appears destined to remain unremarked by her society, she has not only survived; she has prevailed.

3 • For Colored Girls Who Have Considered Suicide When the Rainbow Is Enuf
• The Brothers

Both Ntozake Shange's *For Colored Girls Who Have Considered Suicide When the Rainbow Is Enuf* (1975) and Kathleen Collins's *The Brothers* (1982) portray the interactions of a group of black women. Beyond this surface similarity, however, the two plays form a study in contrasts. In *For Colored Girls*, a loose, nonrealistic structure enables each performer to portray several characters who are united both by their existence in the author's consciousness and by their performance by a single actor. At the same time the performers themselves seem to be participating in a kind of consciousness-raising group, building a feminist community with the other performers onstage that results in a hopeful, forward-looking resolution. In *The Brothers*, a realistic framework of time, place, and character is maintained, within which the secret thoughts and memories of a group of women related by marriage are revealed to the audience—but never to one another. The women's class and color consciousness causes them to isolate themselves from each other, while their passive loyalty to their men drags them down with the men in their doomed struggle to achieve in a racist society.

For Colored Girls began as a performance of poems, dance, and music by Shange and her friends in San Francisco Bayarea bars. The selection of poems and music changed frequently during this period and continued to evolve when the performers took their production to New York. Oz Scott, who became the stage director for the New York opening, suggested final changes to make the performance more theatrical and cohesive. The New York Shakespeare Festival picked up the play after its opening as a workshop in the Henry Street Theatre and moved it to the Public Theatre and finally to the Booth Theatre on Broadway, where it opened to popular acclaim. While most critics praised the play, Stanley Kauffmann commented:

> Most of the pieces seemed to me hyperdramatic and—as writing—superficial, given occasional weight by some skill in presentation and of course by the extra-poetic, extra-theatrical pressure of the subject. That subject is what it's like to grow up black and female in the U.S.

Kauffmann's comment seems at first glance to indicate that the subject is overly theatrical, too theatrical, a somewhat confusing criticism of what is, after all, a theatre piece. Could he mean by "extra-theatrical" that the subject has been treated too often in theatre? Surely not, when the subject is "growing up black and female." On more careful reading, I believe he intends by "extra-theatrical" and "extra-poetic" to condemn the subject as outside the theatrical or the poetic. In other words, Kauffmann says that the subject—"what it's like to grow up black and female in the U.S."—is an inappropriate subject for theatre. This opinion, coming from a major drama reviewer at the *New York Times,* helps to shed some light on the vast silence surrounding that subject in American drama.

The play begins with seven black women running onto stage and freezing "in postures of distress." Each is dressed in a different color. The lady in brown calls to the lady in red, who makes no response. The lady in brown then speaks the opening lines of *For Colored Girls:*

somebody/anybody
sing a black girl's song
bring her out . . .
sing the song of her possibilities (2)

For Colored Girls is thus immediately and explicitly dedicated
to giving voice to silenced women. In the opening speeches of
the play, black women's isolation and powerlessness are expressed in terms of unheard voices: "another song with no
singers: Lyrics / no voices: & interrupted solos: unseen
performances" (1). The colored girl has been "closed in
silence so long / she doesn't know the sound / of her own
voice . . . sing the song of her possibilities / sing a righteous
gospel" (2).

As the play unfolds in the speech of the seven performers,
these contrasting terms of song and silence are developed in
clusters of related images. The play's title itself contains this
tension, contrasting the literal despair of suicide with the hope
symbolized by the rainbow. As the play develops, silence and
the self-hatred of suicide are related to the oppression of
black women by black men, and to the isolation of urban,
technological society. The association between isolation and
technology is first made in "abortion cycle #1." The speaker
describes her isolated situation: "i cdnt have my friends see
this . . . this hurts me: & nobody came: cuz nobody knew: once
i was pregnant and shamed of myself" (17). Her situation is
described in terms of "tubes, tables . . . metal horses gnawin
my womb . . . steel rods," all representing the sterile and
disapproving technological society. In a later poem, the connection between sterility and the white patriarchal society is
reinforced:

we deal wit emotion too much
so why don't we go on ahead & be white then
& make everythin dry & abstract wit no rhythm & no
reelin for sheer sensual pleasure (35)

Finally, the speaker drops her ironic tone to condemn such abstraction as "empty."

White society, however, is not the only nor the most direct oppressor. The stifling world described by the lady in blue in which "i can ride anywhere: remaining a stranger" is Harlem, and the feared oppressor might be "a tall short black brown young man fulla his power" (29). In the poem, "latent rapists," the rapist may be an acquaintance of the victim: "these men friends of ours: who smile nice: stay employed: an take us out to dinner" (14). If such an acquaintance should commit rape, his victim will find it hard to press charges: "a rapist is always to be a stranger: to be legitimate: someone you never saw: a man with obvious problems" (13). Because of this belief, the rapist acts in relative safety, knowing that society's reasoning will be: "if you know him: you must have wanted it" (12). In the isolation of urban society, women's bodies become depersonalized, available for exploitation by "friends" who know they are safe from reprisal.

The racist society has worn away at black women's self-esteem by denigrating their appearance. The play's opening statement observes that "the black girl . . . doesn't know . . . her infinite beauty" (2). In "Sechita," the societal condemnation of black women's appearance is parodied in the description of Sechita's mirror:

> the broken mirror she
> used to decorate her face/made her forehead tilt backwards/
> her cheeks appear sunken/her sassy chin only large enuf/
> to keep her full lower lip/from growin into her neck/sechita/
> had learned to make allowances for the distortions (18)

Sechita's mirror is the mirror of society which distorts the black woman's appearance even in her own eyes: she becomes a Neanderthal type with sloping forehead, giant lips, and no chin. Later in the play, the lady in purple fears she has been rejected by her lover because of her physical appearance:

"Here / : is what i have / : poems / big thighs / lil tits / &: so much love / will you take it from me this one time" (35).

These images of oppression are summed up in the suspenseful climax of the play, "a nite with beau willie brown," recounted by the woman in red. Beau Willie, back from Vietnam, is hiding out from the police in his hometown where his two children live with Crystal, their mother. Beau Willie has been barred from visiting the family after repeated acts of violence toward them, but he goes to their apartment and eventually coaxes Crystal into letting him hold the children. When he has them, he holds them out the fifth-story window, threatening to drop them unless Crystal promises to marry him. Before she can speak, he lets the children fall.

The urban ugliness of Beau Willie's life and the evil effects of his Vietnam experiences are vividly described in the poem, as are Crystal's desperate circumstances as a poor, unmarried mother. It is in fact Crystal's hunger for love and approval that leads her to give the children to Willie: "he coaxed her / tol her she waz . . . pretty & strong . . . beau willie oozed kindness &: crystal who had known so lil / let beau hold [the baby]" (47). The oppressive forces of the racist, sexist hierarchy are held as much responsible for the children's death as Beau Willie, who is merely too weak to overcome these forces in himself.

Nevertheless, the play as a whole portrays black men in a negative light, as the constantly disappointing lovers, the failed intimates of these women. "Ever since i realised there waz someone callt: a colored girl an evil woman a bitch or a nag: i been tryin not to be that & leave bitterness: in somebody else's cup / come to somebody to love me," says the lady in orange. But "i don't know i dont know any more tricks: i am really colored & really sad sometimes & you hurt me" (34-35). It is the failure of the men, as of the rest of society, to love these women for themselves that dooms their relationships. The men have borrowed the attitudes and behavior of white patriarchal society. Bell Hooks, in *Ain't I a Woman?* observes,

Black leaders, male and female, have been unwilling to
acknowledge black male sexist oppression of black wom-
en because they do not want to acknowledge that racism
is not the only oppressive force in our lives. Nor do they
wish to complicate efforts to resist racism by acknowl-
edging that black men can be victimized by racism but at
the same time act as sexist oppressors of black women.
Consequently there is little acknowledgment of sexist
oppression in black male/female relationships as a serious problem. Exaggerated emphasis on the impact of
racism on black men has evoked an image of the black
male as effete, emasculated, crippled. And so intensely
does this image dominate American thinking that people
are absolutely unwilling to admit that the damaging effect
of racism on black men neither prevents them from being
sexist oppressors nor excuses or justifies their sexist
oppression of black women. (88)

Opposing the cluster of oppressive images in the play is one
that relates the beauty of nature and of black women themselves to a pantheistic spirituality based on self-love, sororal
love, and communal expression through song and dance. The
women in the poems combat their oppression and preserve
their self-esteem by singing and dancing: "we gotta dance to
keep from dyin" (11), they say, and "when i can dance like that
/ theres nothin cd hurt me" (33).

Song and dance are constantly related to myth and religion.
The lady in purple describes how, before she fell in love and
became vulnerable to a man, she "lived wit myths & music was
my old man & i cd dance: a dance outta time" (34). "Sechita"
portrays a dance hall girl with her roots in "quadroon balls/
elegance in st. louis," and even more ancient ones in the
"egyptian goddess of creativity/second millenium" (18). Sechita
also lives with myths, using dance to defy her situation:

her calf was tauntin the brazen carnie
lights/the full moon/sechita/goddess of love/egypt
second millenium/performin the rites/the conjurin of
men
conjurin the spirit (19)

Sechita's spirituality has nothing to do with Christianity. She identifies herself with an Egyptian goddess and is eager to leave dusty Natchez where a male "god seemed to be wipin his feet in her face" (19). Her beliefs are both pantheistic and matriarchal, based, as ancient matriarchal religions were, on worship of the moon. The rite she performs is "the conjurin of men," suggesting a pre-Christian unity of sexuality with spirituality. A later poem explicitly describes a "godliness [which] is plenty is ripe & fertile" (35), and elsewhere the lady in yellow proclaims that "my soul is too ancient to understand the separation of soul & gender" (36). Thus, the spirituality that develops in the play is a matriarchal, pantheistic religion that does not separate body and soul either to oppress women or to condemn sexuality.

The final section of the play, in which all the performers participate, is entitled "a layin on of hands," suggesting a shared religious gesture of blessing and healing. The lady in purple says that the laying on of hands will be "the holiness of myself released" (50), implying a spirituality based on self-esteem. The poem begins, "i waz missing somethin," something that is "free," "pure," that is not "layin on bodies" or "mama / holdin me tight" but a haunting need, "the ghost of another woman / who waz missin what I waz missin" (48-50). Nature offers the women comfort in a tree that "took me up in her branches: held me in the breeze: made me dawn dew: that chill at daybreak: the sun wrapped me up swingin rose light everywhere" (50). All the actresses say and then sing the words, "i found god in myself: & i loved her: i loved her fiercely" (51). The actresses "enter into a closed tight circle" and the play ends with the lady in brown saying again, "& this is for colored girls who have considered: suicide / but are movin to the end of their own: rainbows" (51). The beauty of nature, represented in the sun, the trees, and the rainbow, comforts the women and enables them to begin to love themselves. The final poem and song suggest a communal form of worship based on an experience of transcendent nature, self-acceptance, and sororal love.

Clearly, community is central to *For Colored Girls*. The play, originally a collection of Shange's poems, has no one protagonist unless it is Shange herself. While some poems portray specific, named characters, these characters are usually described in the third person, suggesting that the performer is a storyteller rather than the character herself. Many of the other poems, written in the first person, seem to be the personal, lyric expressions of Shange, who even refers to herself by name in "somebody almost walked off wid alla my stuff": "this is mine / ntozake 'her own things' / that's my name" (39). Thus, while the audience is clearly intended to see in each poem a different woman in specific circumstances, it is also invited to see each character as an aspect of Shange's personality, or as her creation.

Further, because each of the eight performers represents several characters, the performer retains a greater presence as herself onstage than do actors in a realistic drama. As the women confide what seem to be their own experiences as well as other women's stories to one another and to the audience, they seem to be developing a sense of feminist community onstage during the performance. In the absence of a conventional plot, it is this growing sense of a feminist community among the performers that gives the play its momentum.

At the beginning of the play, each actress is isolated in her own spotlight. As she speaks, the others form an audience that gradually becomes involved in commenting on the stories. The performers dance together, tease each other, and offer each other sympathy and advice. At one point, they take turns describing their lovers' favorite apologies for infidelity:

> LADY IN YELLOW: get this, last week my ol man came in sayin, "i don't know how she got yr number baby, i'm sorry"
>
> LADY IN BROWN: no this one is it, "o baby, ya know i waz high, i'm sorry." (41)

The performers' developing sense of community through

shared experiences is suggestive of feminist consciousness-raising groups of the seventies. As in a c-r group, these are women who deliberately share their lives in an effort to understand the nature of their oppression and develop a sense of feminist sisterhood. Gerda Lerner, in defining feminist consciousness, describes the following stages of development:

> 1) the awareness of a wrong; 2) the development of a sense of sisterhood; 3) the autonomous definition by women of their goals and strategies for changing their condition, and 4) the development of an alternate vision of the future. (*Patriarchy*, 242)

This is the process the performers themselves seem to undergo in the course of *For Colored Girls,* culminating in the final poem's vision of a communal feminist future.

Honor Moore calls *For Colored Girls* a "choral play," that is, one which "shows us women together, women seeking integration by attempting community," as opposed to one type of "autonomous woman play" in which "the protagonist is divided into several selves each of whom expresses different versions of the woman in question" (186-187). But *For Colored Girls* seems to function in both ways, showing many different women's experiences but pointing up the similarities that underlie them, and including not only the characters, but the performers and the playwright in the community of "colored girls" to whom the play is dedicated.

While the community represented in the play is limited to women and to women of color, there seem to be no barriers of class or ethnicity within this group. One poem is a celebration of Latin music by a young woman who cheerfully explains that "my papa thot he was puerto rican & we wda been: cept we waz just reglar niggas wit hints of spanish . . . wit my colored new jersey self: didn't know what anybody waz saying: cept if dancin waz proof of origin: I was jibarita herself" (8). The social class of the characters ranges from the bookish middle-class child in "toussaint" to the young, unmarried mother living in a fifth-floor tenement in "beau willie." In reality, many of the women described would never meet. The community of the play, based on shared racist and sexist oppression, does not exist on a realistic plane but on a spiritual one. The play's resolution looks optimistically toward a future in which women of color will affirm themselves and one another, thus gaining the strength to transform the oppressive society.

The Brothers, winner of an NEA Playwriting Grant and selected by the Theatre Communications Group as one of twelve outstanding new plays of the season, had its premiere at the American Place Theatre on March 31, 1982. Critical response was encouraging; Frank Rich of the *New York Times* called Kathleen Collins "a promising writer . . . capable of passions both tender and angry." In July of 1982, Collins revised the play, eliminating the only two male characters.

Most mainstream drama, of course, revolves around the lives of men. *The Brothers* as a title heightens audience expectations that this will be another such play. But ironically, although the characters' lives revolve around the brothers of the title, the men never appear onstage. *The Brothers* takes place in "The living room of Danielle Edwards' house; adjacent spaces that exist in the minds and memories of the characters" (300). As this description suggests, the play is nominally realistic, but characters engage in soliloquies and flashbacks, opening out the realistic structure. The characters, all women, are united only by their relationships to the Edwards brothers. Danielle is the wife of Nelson Edwards, Caroline is the wife of Lawrence Edwards, and Lillie and Letitia are the first and second wives of Franklin Edwards. Marietta is the Edwards's unmarried sister, and Rosie is Lillie's mother. A fourth Edwards brother, Jeremy, lives in Chicago with his wife Aurora, who does not appear onstage.

From the first moment of the play, when we see Lillie waiting for the doctor's diagnosis of Nelson's disease, to the last scene spent waiting for Nelson's funeral to begin, the women almost never initiate an action. Instead, they react to the brothers who, as described in flashbacks, had been ambitious, hardworking young men filled with a drive to achieve in the white world when they married. Each brother represents a different realm of achievement: Nelson, athletics; Franklin, religion and education; Lawrence, business. Only the stammering Jeremy has opted out of the struggle to be among "the first of the first of the coloreds," by moving away and taking a job in a slaughterhouse. The rest of the Edwards family is engaged in a life-and-death struggle to enter the upper classes of American society.

The play opens on Lillie alone: "A stunning woman around 30, she is fair enough to pass for white" (301). The date is February 1, 1948; the radio news announces the assassination of Gandhi. The "old-maidish" Marietta comes down from Nelson's bedroom (always referred to as the Upper Room) to tell Lillie that Nelson, although he suffers only from minor asthma, refuses to leave his bed. Nelson, an Olympic runner, has decided that "negro life is a void," and will spend the next twenty years of his life bedridden, in increasingly childish dependence on his wife and the other women in the family.

Nelson's wife, Danielle, emerges next from the Upper Room. She is "around 27, stunning too but without LILLIE'S polished grace" (303). Danielle reports that Lillie's husband, Franklin, is praying with Nelson, and mockingly imitates Nelson's style of prayer. Lillie is amused, but Marietta is shocked and disapproving. Lillie, who writes humorous poetry herself, defends Danielle's parody saying, "They call it poetic license, Marietta, truth in the form of free-fallen verse" (305). In a flashback, Marietta recalls hearing about Lillie from Franklin for the first time, and worrying that Lillie might not approve of her. "I'm not subtle or delicate as I suspect her to be. She's not been raised around four boys all her life . . . pushing and pulling and tugging at me . . . till sometimes I feel like an abrupt male thing . . . who am I anyway . . . am I just you boys' shadow that no one will ever see?" (311).

Danielle, who has exited upstairs, returns to report that Nelson refuses to leave bed even to use the toilet. She adds that Franklin has asked Nelson, "what would we do if the whole race went back to bed," and she and Lillie begin to laugh hysterically at the notion of "armies of Negroes taking to their beds. . . . Declaring Nelson King of the Void." But Danielle adds more seriously, "which makes me what . . . Queen of the Bed Pans . . . [She can't help wincing.] . . . that's kind of hard to get dressed up for. [Suddenly frightened.] I could lose my bearings, Lillie. I'm only built for speed" (313). The act ends with Marietta screaming from upstairs that Nelson is trying to suffocate himself with his bed pillow.

Act 2, scene 1, four months later, opens on Danielle overheard talking to Nelson, who is still in bed. "Just get up and go to work!" she tells him. "We could have a few drinks, a few kids, *then* you can die" (315). Her unanswered conversation with Nelson becomes a soliloquy as she comes down the stairs:

> This could get bleak . . . me, a bottle of gin and a looney-tune colored man. [That makes her laugh in spite of herself.] Colored or not, I'm not built for despair . . . must be a high yaller impulse to keep things light. I'm descended from too long a line of sallow women who taught me to look stylish and shut my mouth . . . wear my skin like it was a precious jewel . . . wait for choice negro offerings to line up at my door. . . . It was not my intention to think life through! Wind up with answers that lead nowhere but down! (316)

A phone call reveals that a family dinner party is planned. Danielle exits to the Upper Room to tend Nelson, and Caroline enters, "a woman in her mid 30's, exquisitely dressed in an expensive fur coat that fits her to perfection" (316). In a flashback, Caroline recalls meeting her husband, Lawrence, a businessman and deal maker: "I'm standing on a cool balcony on a hot summer night. . . . I refuse to go down and sweat with the crowd. I look too good . . . all of a sudden, Lawrence walks in" (319). Marietta recalls her brothers' disapproval of her prospective suitors. Speaking to Franklin in memory, she says, "you mock anyone who comes near my door . . . [Mimicking him.] 'He's not good enough for you, Marietta, not that scrawny negro fool.' [They laugh] . . . you're as bad as Pop . . . will he be among the first of the first of the coloreds, he'd say . . . [They begin to giggle.]" (320). Caroline managed to find a husband who is "above the crowd." Because Marietta did not, she is forced to remain single.

The scene shifts to Rosie's home, where Lillie is staying during an illness. Lillie longs to recover and go home to her husband, Franklin, a mortician. "If I were home, I could answer the phone for my Frankie Boy, tell him who died . . . someone's dead, we can pay our bills, go out to dinner, have a night on the town, we're rich, Frankie Boy, look at the pleasures death will loan us for an hour!" (322). In a flashback, she recalls that Franklin's ambition was to become a teacher. "You'll make a wonderful teacher," she told him, "eager, upstanding, stern to a fault" (323). Franklin, however, has remained a mortician, moonlighting as a night watchman. The act ends with Lillie's unexpected collapse and death. Thinking of Danielle, Lillie cries:

> don't let their pride defeat you, it's a sickness, they're all too angry to breathe . . . [With sudden defiance.] I will NOT live off of anger, dead bodies, defeated dreams! Watch my Frankie Boy brood on all the unfair negro things.

Her dying words are "flowers *burst* into bloom, Momma, all of a sudden they thrust themselves free!" (326).

In the short second scene of act 2, Caroline arrives to tend Nelson while the family goes to Lillie's funeral. In a flashback, she recalls herself telling her husband:

> you should've all been born white, you spend your lives trying to jump out of your skin . . . [That amuses her but makes Lawrence turn mean. She imitates him.] "Listen to the maid . . . got five cents' worth of education and she's tryin' out ideas . . ." [As herself.] Stop saying that! That's how you got through all those schools!" (331)

She reveals that she is expecting a child, and hopes that it will
"breathe something new between us." Her reverie is shattered
by Nelson, thumping on the floor for help. Caroline starts for
the Upper Room, saying, "What's the matter with you . . .
what's the matter with *all* of you! You think we're a bunch of
bleeding stagehands!" (332) as the second act ends.

Act 3 takes place on April 5, 1968, the day of Nelson's
funeral, and the day after the assassination of Martin Luther
King. Letitia, Franklin's second wife, looks back on her loveless marriage and concludes, "I did not leave . . . I think that is
my great accomplishment, that I did not leave" (340). The
widow, Danielle, is drinking heavily. Caroline arrives without
Lawrence, admitting, "He's been gone all night, he's gone a lot
of nights. . . . It'll be the same old story . . . a sudden real estate
deal, legal tie-ups that lasted through the night. [She shakes
her head disbelieving.]" (343-344). She fears it is the death of
their daughter, Laura, that keeps him away from home.

In a final flashback, Danielle reveals that her husband's
death, supposed to be the result of a fatal asthma attack, was in
reality murder. Recalling his constant weeping and questioning "why [whites] think we're dumb or different or inhuman,"
she finally "goes out of control":

> Stop it, stop acting like a baby! I'll have to leave the
> planet if you don't cut out this act! [Then with real
> violence, she acts it out.] Stop it, I say, or I'll drown you
> my own self, hold this pillow over you till you're blue in
> the face . . . [Which she does, pressing it down harder
> and harder until death stops his tears and her own can
> start.] (346)

Marietta concludes the play with her discovery of one of
Lillie's doggerel verses, written twenty years before and kept
under Nelson's pillow:

> Gandhi's dead
> so I said
> She only turned and stared

> Nelson's in bed
> so she said
> I only laughed and glared
> Gandhi's dead
> I said again
> What's that to me, she replied
> Nelson's in bed
> Again she said
> All colored men do is die. (346)

Like *For Colored Girls, The Brothers* brings a group of black women who have been, in Caroline's words, "bleeding stage managers," to center stage. Although the women in *The Brothers* are uniformly elevated in social status, they lead a marginal existence in the shadows of their men. Unlike the performers in *For Colored Girls,* they never proclaim their right to a more central status; instead, the playwright dramatizes their secret thoughts without permitting them to share these with each other. Although they are all related by blood or by marriage, the women in *The Brothers* never develop a sense of community, nor do they transcend their circumstances to move to the center of their own lives. Instead, they spend their lives waiting in attendance on the men.

Barbara Christian observes in *Black Feminist Criticism* that the concept of class is

> a major factor upon which the societal norm of what a woman is supposed to be is based. Just as blacks as a group were relegated to an underclass in America by virtue of their race, so women were relegated to a separate caste by virtue of their sex. But within that separate caste, a standard of woman was designed in terms of a class definition. (72)

Christian describes this standard or ideal American woman as beautiful and fair-skinned, chastely married, and a mother. The woman who fulfills this ideal does not work outside the home but provides comforts for her intelligent, aggressive husband, who achieves in the outside world. Black women,

Christian notes, have usually had to work to support themselves and their families, and often cannot conform to the
white standard of beauty. Yet as women they have been
denied the opportunity to compete aggressively in the work
world. "On one hand, they could not achieve the standard of
womanhood; on the other hand, they were biologically females, with all the societal restrictions associated with that
state" (72).

The Edwards wives, because they were light-skinned and
beautiful, believed they could avoid this double bind and
marry ambitious, successful black men who would support
them in passive luxury. They expected to achieve the standard
that Christian describes. But racism ultimately defeats even
the talented, ambitious Edwards brothers and, through them,
their wives. Nelson, his Olympic running career slowed by age
and asthma, succumbs first and most dramatically. Franklin
remains a mortician, never finishing college. Lawrence's business deals are described as increasingly shady; some are simply
fictions to cover loveless extramarital affairs.

Because the men have failed to achieve, the women who
have defined themselves only in relation to their men are also
failures. In Danielle's final soliloquy, she recalls Nelson's
asking her why she has remained with him so long. She
answers:

> because I was too lazy, I guess to lift myself up . . . instead
> I sat around with you . . . let time go backwards on me . . .
> let your grieving get into my bones, like damp chill . . .
> then I drifted inside your shadow the way women can do
> . . . next think I know I've been sitting here for years . . .
> soaked clean through on the thin excuses you exchanged
> for a life. (345)

Danielle is bitter because the life of glamour and luxury she
expected from marriage to Nelson never materialized. By the
opening scene of the play, Nelson has already decided that
because of racism, their ambitions are "futile . . . that negro

life is a void" (302). This realization gradually spreads through the Edwards family in the twenty-year span of the play, spawning alcoholism, infidelity, and finally murder.

The characters exist in a suffocating isolation. Much of the play is made up of soliloquies and flashbacks presented as monologues; conversation between the women is mostly meaningless small talk. As in other respects, Nelson represents the most extreme form of this silence, refusing eventually to speak at all. Instead, he pounds on the floor for attention, and then writes notes. He symbolically attempts suicide by pressing a pillow to his face as if to silence himself, and his disease is asthma, which has the primary symptom of shortness of breath. Finally, his death is by suffocation at the hands of his wife.

The effort to achieve in isolation and even in competition with other people of color, to be "the first of the first among the coloreds" has been the Edwards family's only response to racism. The mention of Gandhi and Martin Luther King reminds the audience that other communal responses exist. The characters seem, however, to have dismissed all such group efforts. While Franklin prays with Nelson, and the references to the Upper Room make a clear comparison between Nelson and Jesus, both martyred by their societies, the family members do not seem to be church goers. No ministers or church members show up to offer support in times of illness or death.

Similarly, the family participates in politics but seems to avoid any identification with their racial group. Letitia predicts that Franklin, an assemblyman, will be asked to speak on King's death.

> He'll say something gracious, though he'll be mad as can be. I can hear him now . . . [Speaking like FRANKLIN.] "Just because I'm the only . . . [She has a hard time saying the word.] . . . Black, they'll expect me to speak . . . like I was the spokesman for Negro grief." [She sighs.] He hates the race stuff politics locks him into. (335)

Marietta's response to the news of King's death is, "Maybe Nelson was right to have slept through it all" (335). In the minds of the family, Gandhi's and King's accomplishments are completely negated by their deaths. The play concludes at the time when the second wave of women's liberation in the U.S. was gaining force, but the characters make no mention of this movement either.

Nor do the women turn to each other for communal support, despite their proximity and the similarity of their circumstances. Like the ideal patriarchal wife described by Christian, they owe allegiance entirely to their husbands and brothers and regard one another with suspicion. Thus, without communal support of any kind, the characters are doomed to total isolation, a kind of life-in-death from which no escape seems possible.

Images of death permeate *The Brothers*. The play is framed by the deaths of Gandhi and Martin Luther King. Franklin works as a mortician, and lives with Lillie and their children in the funeral home. Jeremy works in a slaughterhouse. Lillie and Nelson die in the course of the play, and Carolyn's daughter is reported only as an expected birth, and then as an untimely death. The final words of the play, quoted from the dead Lillie's poem to the dead Nelson—"all colored men do is die"—scarcely seems an exaggeration.

The Brothers and *For Colored Girls* present two sides of the same coin: a group of black women living in suffocating isolation within the patriarchy, and a group of black women struggling to overcome patriarchal oppression through feminist community. While *The Brothers* was written later than *For Colored Girls,* it depicts an earlier era in history, and relates its story through flashbacks. *For Colored Girls* presents a moment in contemporary history, and manages to suggest that the performers themselves are being transformed into a community at the present moment of performance, projecting an optimistic, almost utopian vision of the future.

Both plays express a similar disappointment in heterosexual romance, and neither opens the possibility of lesbian romance. The women in *The Brothers* had hoped to live out a romantic ideal as the pampered, passive brides of achieving men, but the racist society has dashed this hope. In the ultimate antiromantic resolution, Nelson's wife murders him over her disappointment. While this is certainly not a comic resolution, it lacks the cathartic effect of tragedy as well. Thus, it, too, is an open-ended play.

Although the plays contrast in subject and style, they reinforce each other in thematic content. *The Brothers* shows the living death imposed on its characters by their stubborn loyalty to the patriarchy's racist, classist isolation. *For Colored Girls,* as its title suggests, shows the possibility of overcoming suicidal self-hatred through the realization of feminist community represented by the rainbow, ancient symbol of hope.

4 • *Getting Out*
  • *'Night, Mother*

Only a few years ago, Heide Gottner-Abendroth observed
that "in patriarchal societies aesthetics is divided into a formalist,
elitist, socially effective art on the one hand, and a popular,
widespread but socially vilified and outcast art on the other."
She went on to argue that feminist art transcend this division
in order to "return art to its original public role" (563). I would
argue that feminist drama has already begun this process. All
the playwrights considered in this book have achieved some
measure of critical and commercial success; all can be considered feminist. Even in this group, however, Marsha Norman
stands out as perhaps the most successful author of serious
feminist drama working in the U.S. today.

Norman's first play, *Getting Out*, was produced in 1977 as
part of the Festival of New American Playwrights at the
Actors Theatre in Louisville, where it was recognized as "the
best entry in the festival" (Eder). It was subsequently produced at the Mark Taper Forum and in New York at the
Theater de Lys. It received the John Gassner Medallion, the
Newsday Oppenheimer Award, and the American Theater
Critics Citation as Best New Play in Regional Theaters. Her
second play, *'Night, Mother*, had its premiere at the American
Repertory Theater in Cambridge, Massachusetts, in 1982, and
opened on Broadway in 1983 for an extended run. *'Night*,

Mother received the Susan Smith Blackburn Prize and the 1983 Pulitzer Prize for Drama, and has been made into a film. Norman's critical and commercial success, even at this early point in her career, is indisputable, yet her plays grapple with difficult subjects, approached from a viewpoint that clearly reflects both female psychology and a feminist ethic.

In *Getting Out*, Arlene, a young woman recently released from prison, struggles with the help of her upstairs neighbor Ruby to establish a new life "on the outside" for herself and eventually, she hopes, her son. In *'Night, Mother*, Jessie, a divorced, unemployed woman living with her mother, has decided to commit suicide. In the course of the play, Jessie attempts to explain this decision to her mother and to release her from responsibility either for Jessie's life or for her decision to end it. In both plays, women who have been silenced by the patriarchal society break their silence in order to claim their autonomy. In each case, however, it is an autonomy in connection for which the women struggle.

As Jean Baker Miller describes, "Women are quite validly seeking something more complete than autonomy as it is defined for men, a fuller not a lesser ability to encompass relationships to others, simultaneously with the fullest development of oneself" (95). Miller argues that the terms "autonomy" and even "ego" may not be entirely appropriate in describing female psychology, since women often believe that they exist only to serve other people's needs.

Nancy Chodorow believes that this sense of existence only in connection arises largely because women are almost universally the primary nurturing figures for infants and small children. Boys therefore grow to define themselves in separation from primary parents of the opposite sex—their mothers—while girls continue to feel strongly connected to their mothers and eventually to family and community. Carol Gilligan describes the conflict that can result between a woman's desire to serve others and her need to help herself. When this is resolved by an understanding that the needs of self and others are interwoven, the result is what Gilligan calls an "ethic of care." In *Getting Out* and in *'Night, Mother,* the protagonists struggle to achieve autonomy in connection, to define themselves with integrity but in relation to others. In *'Night, Mother,* these others are reduced to the child's one essential other, Jessie's mother. In *Getting Out,* Arlene confronts a community of others as well as her own past self, and struggles to find the appropriate response to each.

The setting of *Getting Out* is the "dingy, one-room apartment in a rundown section of downtown Louisville, Kentucky," which Arlene has "inherited" from a sister. "A catwalk stretches above the apartment and a prison cell . . . connects to it by stairways. . . . The apartment must seem imprisoned," the stage directions explain (5). Two actresses portray the protagonist: one, Arlene, inhabits the apartment in present time, and the other, Arlie, "the violent kid Arlene was until her last stretch in prison," moves through the apartment at times, unseen by the other characters, but primarily inhabits the catwalk and prison cell in the past.

Arlie appears first, with a funny, slightly ghoulish story about throwing a neighbor boy's frogs into the street to be run over by cars. Arlene then arrives with Bennie, a retired prison guard who admired Arlie's "wild cat" ways in solitary confinement, and who has driven her to her new apartment. When Bennie leaves to get dinner, Arlene is visited first by her mother, a hard-bitten cab driver who devotes her visit to cleaning the apartment while making it clear that Arlene will no longer be welcome in her home; then by her former pimp, Carl, who hopes to persuade her to return to prostitution. Arlene's attention to her visitors is constantly interrupted by memories enacted by Arlie and a series of guards, teachers, and peers from her childhood and adolescence in schools, reformatories, and prisons.

While Arlene and her mother talk and clean, Arlie reveals in a flashback that she was sexually molested by her father. While Carl describes the easy life on the streets to Arlene, Arlie recalls, "You always sendin me to them ol' droolers. . . . They slobberin all over me . . . They tyin me to the bed! . . . I

could git killed workin for you" (33). Bennie's return drives
Carl away, and Arlene explains that Carl is the father of Joey,
the baby she bore in prison who is now a little boy living in
foster homes. While Bennie and Arlene eat, Arlie sits in
prison rocking her pillow, expressing her passionate love for
the baby she has never known. After dinner, Bennie attempts
first to seduce Arlene and then, when she rejects him, forces
her onto the bed. She tries at first to fight him off as Arlie
would have done, but finally stops him by calling him a rapist.
Shocked, Bennie retreats as act 1 ends.

Act 2 begins with Arlene asleep while Arlie enacts her time
in solitary confinement broken only by tormenting guards and
a sympathetic prison chaplain. Arlene is awake and making a
grocery list when Ruby comes to the door. Ruby reveals that
she is also an ex-convict, and offers the use of her phone and
the possibility of a job at the coffee shop where she cooks.
Arlene is suspicious, however, and a flashback shows Arlie
warding off sexual advances by prison inmates. After Ruby
leaves, a flashback shows Bennie's friendly but paternalistic
relationship with Arlie in prison, and covers the passage of
present time until Arlene returns with a bag of groceries.
When the bag breaks, Arlene collapses on the floor, momentarily despairing. Carl returns, and this time makes his argument on economic grounds: "You can do cookin and cleanin
OR you can do somethin that pays good. You ain't gonna git
rich working on your knees. You come with me an you'll have
money. You stay here, you won't have shit" (56). Arlene is
determined to go straight and win custody of Joey, however,
and Carl becomes hostile at her rejection. His shouting draws
Ruby to the door and Carl goes, leaving a phone number
where Arlene can reach him.

Arlene now confesses to Ruby how she escaped solitary
confinement and eventually prison. She had become close to
the prison chaplain, who called her Arlene and assured her
that "Arlie was my hateful self and she was hurtin me and God
would find some way to take her away" (61). When the
chaplain was unexpectedly transferred, Arlene suffered an

emotional breakdown. She was found in her cell, stabbing herself repeatedly with a fork and saying, "Arlie is dead for what she done to me, Arlie is dead an it's God's will" (61). She came to consciousness in the hospital and, under the gentle treatment she received, believed she had succeeded in "killing" her delinquent self. She reformed her behavior, learned to knit, and became the best housekeeper in her dorm. Now, however, she is surrounded again by people calling her "Arlie" and by situations that seem to demand her old, violent behavior. She breaks down, crying, "Arlie!" and the stage directions indicate she is "grieving for this lost self" (62). Ruby comforts her, saying, "you can still love people that's gone," and rocking her "as with a baby."

Bennie returns briefly with apologies and plants to decorate the apartment, and leaves a phone number with Arlene as well. When he is gone, Arlene stands weighing the two phone numbers—Bennie's and Carl's—finally tearing up Carl's and offering to play cards with Ruby—Old Maids, the only game she knows. The play ends with another monologue by Arlie, in which she recalls being locked into a closet by her sister. She responded by peeing in her mother's shoes, an action Arlie and Arlene now laugh about together. They speak in unison, recalling the mother's reaction, "Arlie, what you doin in there?" and it is clear that Arlene has reclaimed her love for Arlie, her lost child self.

At the beginning of the play Arlene has begun the transition from silence to speech. Arlie, silenced by her father, locked in the closet by her sister, could only express her anger physically, bringing increasingly serious punishments on herself in a deadly downward spiral. "I'm not Arlie," Arlene tells Bennie bitterly as he abandons his attempted rape. "Arlie coulda killed you." Arlene learns to use speech instead, first as her defense against Bennie, then as her connection with Ruby, and finally, through Ruby's supportive sisterhood, as a way to reunite with Arlie and speak as one, complete person—a delightfully exuberant and mischievous person at that.

Like Arlene, Jessie in 'Night, Mother is a woman silenced by society. She can't hold a job; she found a husband only through her mother's machinations and then lost him again. She is without beauty, talent, or popularity. Unlike Arlene, though, she has been less oppressed than simply overlooked by the patriarchal society. She even appears to have played into this invisibility, rarely leaving the house and avoiding her brother, Dawson, and his family. She is closest to her mother, but seems to have stayed on a surface level even with her until now. When she tells her mother, "You have no earthly idea how I feel," Mama responds, "Well, how could I? You're real far back there, Jessie" (55).

On the evening depicted in the play, Jessie breaks her lifelong silence in order to connect with and console Mama for her planned suicide, which ends the play. *'Night, Mother* is set in the living room, connecting kitchen, and center hall of Mama's home, "a relatively new house built way out on a country road." A bedroom door is visible in the hall, which should be "the focal point of the entire set. . . . It is an ordinary door that opens onto absolute nothingness" (3).

Mama begins the play by searching for snowball cupcakes in the kitchen, establishing the atmosphere of mundane domesticity that is maintained throughout the play. Jessie is also searching the house—for beach towels, rubber sheets, and her father's gun. When she reveals, almost casually, the gun's intended use, Mama reacts at first with disbelief. The remainder of the play is occupied by Mama's attempts to dissuade Jessie and Jessie's corresponding efforts to explain herself, to make sure Mama can run the house without her, and to relieve Mama of responsibility for her death.

Norman has said that she composed the play like a piece of music, in a series of rising and falling movements. Norman did not delineate these movements in detail, and might not agree with the following interpretation, which is my own. Certainly, however, it is possible to detect such a pattern of rising and falling movements in the two women's interactions. The first of these begins with Jessie's revelation of her intention. She asks her mother to accept her plan, to spend the evening visiting with her and not to call Jessie's brother, Dawson, for help. When Jessie leaves the room and Mama considers calling Dawson but decides against it, the first movement ends. In the second movement, Mama tries to find a concrete reason for Jessie's decision, so she can refute it. Certainly Jessie's epilepsy, her divorce, and her delinquent son, Ricky, are factors, but to Jessie, the decision is simpler and less self-pitying than this welter of circumstances would suggest. She compares her life to a bus ride:

> hot and bumpy and crowded and too noisy and more than anything in the world you want to get off and the only reason in the world you don't get off is it's still fifty blocks from where you're going? Well, I can get off right now if I want to, because even if I ride fifty more years and get off then, it's the same place when I step down to it. (33)

Jessie hopes her mother will simply accept this and let Jessie "ask you things I always wanted to know and you could make me some hot chocolate. The old way" (36). Again, Mama accedes, ending the second movement in the activity of making hot chocolate.

In the third movement, Jessie attempts to find out from her mother things she has always wondered: Why doesn't Mama's friend Agnes visit the house? Did her mother love her father? Agnes, it turns out, is frightened by Jessie's cold hands. Jessie's mother didn't love her father, now dead, and Mama confesses to jealousy of the closeness Jessie and her father had shared. In return, Mama wants to know why Jessie's husband, Cecil, left her. Jessie can only speculate that it was for the same reason she fell off a horse when Cecil tried, early in their marriage, to teach her to ride: she didn't know how to hold on. Tying up the trash bag, Jessie explains that Carl would not take Jessie when he left town because "you don't pack your garbage when you move" (61), thus ending the movement.

Jessie has always believed that the fall from the horse brought on her epilepsy, but Mama now reveals that Jessie had epilepsy from childhood, inherited, Mama thinks, from her father. Jessie resents Mama's decision to keep this knowledge from her, but maintains it is not the epilepsy, which in any case is now under control with medication, that has made her decide to die. In the fourth movement, Mama tries to find out in what way she is responsible for Jessie's failed life: "Maybe I fed you the wrong thing. Maybe you had a fever sometime and I didn't know it soon enough. Maybe it's a punishment. . . . It has to be something I did" (71). Jessie insists it is not, and Mama is driven to pleading, "Don't leave me, Jessie!" (72). Jessie goes to get a box of gifts she has prepared for Mama to give people, closing the fourth movement.

In the final movement of the play, Mama pleads with Jessie to live "just a few more years" (74) to keep her mother company, arguing for the value of daily existence and the chance that Jessie's life will improve. Exhilarated by their new intimacy, Mama urges, "We could have more talks like tonight. . . . I'll pay more attention to you. Tell the truth when you ask me. Let you have your say." But Jessie responds, "No, Mama. *This* is how I have my say. This is how I say what I thought about it ALL and I say no. To Dawson and Loretta and the Red Chinese and epilepsy and Ricky and Cecil and you. And me. And hope. I say no!" Paradoxically, Jessie asserts autonomy over her life by making the decision to end it (75).

Jessie makes suggestions to her mother about the funeral, advises her to call Dawson as soon as Jessie is dead and to wash the chocolate pan until he arrives, and shows her the gifts she has prepared. Mama makes a last, futile attempt to restrain Jessie physically, but Jessie goes into her room, saying "'Night, Mother." Mama, weeping at the door, hears the gunshot and says, "Jessie, Jessie, child . . . Forgive me. I thought you were mine" (89). Then she goes to call Dawson, the chocolate pan clutched in her hand.

In both *'Night, Mother* and *Getting Out,* women are presented in domestic interior settings redolent of women's material culture. While homemaking is not quite the sacred activity described by Rabuzzi, it is something of deep significance to the women in Norman's plays. To Arlene, her new apartment is the first space she has ever been able to call her own. Much of the stage business involves her attempt to make a home for herself by arranging her possessions, cleaning, and shopping. Significantly, the domestic becomes the nexus of Arlene's relationship to the other characters. Her mother visits to help her clean, and their only productive conversations revolve around this housework. Bennie urges her to start making her own decisions on how to arrange the apartment and buys her plants to hide the bars on the windows. Carl, on the other hand, breaks down her door, eats her food, and throws groceries on the floor. Finally Ruby offers homespun advice on how to survive independently when pressures mount:

> RUBY: You kin always call in sick . . . stay home, send out for pizza an watch your Johnny Carson on TV . . . or git a bus way out Preston Street and go bowlin. . . .
>
> ARLENE: [anger building] What am I gonna do? . . . What kind of life is that?
>
> RUBY: It's outside. (59)

Ruby here defines freedom as the chance to control where she goes and what she eats. Throughout the play, Arlene's changing attitude to the domestic and especially to food symbolizes her movement toward autonomous selfhood. When Arlie was a child, food was a form of patriarchal control associated with violence and sex. Mama reflects: "You always was too skinny. Shoulda beat you like your daddy said. Make you eat" (19). This is immediately followed by Arlie's revelation to the audience, but not to Mama, that her father molested and beat her. The prison guards try to get Arlie to eat for explicitly sexual reasons: "Got us a two-way mirror in the shower room . . . We sure do care if you go gittin too skinny" (18). In prison the "good girls" obediently ate, and Arlie says that most were fat. Arlie, however, resists violently, flinging her food at the wall. After her breakdown, she gave in to offers of chocolate pudding, and even as she begins her new life, she complies with Bennie's insistence that she eat the chicken he has bought, forcing it down although she claims she isn't hungry.

In act 2, Arlene's increasing commitment to an autonomous existence is shown by her determination to shop for the food she likes to stock her own shelves in her own home. At the play's end, Arlene's determination to make her new life work is clear when, "Slowly but with great determination, she picks up the [grocery] items one at a time and puts them away in the cabinet above the counter." For Arlene, such mundane details are the palpable signs of her autonomy; moreover, they symbolize the new domestic life she plans to establish with her son. Her newly discovered respect for the material culture of cooking and eating reflects her newfound confidence in herself.

In 'Night, Mother, the domestic environment shared by mother and daughter externalizes the bond they share. The question under debate—whether to live or die—is represented for both characters by the value they place on their material surroundings. The play is filled with the stage business of Jessie's domestic preparations for departure. She and Mama wrestle the newly laundered cover back on the sofa; Jessie refills the candy dishes, explains how the washer works, and updates her mother on the procedure for ordering groceries: "And they won't deliver less than fifteen dollars' worth. What I do is tell them to add on cigarettes until it gets to fifteen dollars" (25). Just as Ruby offers Arlene the power to send out for pizza as a reason for living "straight," so Mama tries to dissuade Jessie from suicide by suggesting: "You could work some puzzles or put in a garden or go to the store. Let's call a taxi and go to the A & P!" (34). To Mama gardening, shopping for food, and eating represent reasons to live. But although Jessie recognizes her mother's pleasure, it is not a pleasure she can share.

Near the end of the play, Jessie tries one last time to explain why she wants to die: "I would wonder, sometimes, what might keep me here, what might be worth staying for, and you know what it was? It was maybe if there was something I really liked, like maybe if I really liked rice pudding or cornflakes for breakfast or something, that might be enough" (77). Unlike Arlene, who decides to put away the groceries and begin a new life, Jessie finds no pleasure in eating and thus no reason to live. Jessie's rejection of Mama's life of domesticity is, in the terms of the play, a rejection of life itself.

In both plays, the protagonists struggle within this domestic environment to define themselves autonomously. In *Getting Out,* Arlie's struggles form the ongoing "plot" of the flashbacks. Arlie is trapped in a series of figurative or literal prisons in the course of the play: first by her father, then by Carl, and finally by the prison guards. Even the reformed Arlene is still in a kind of prison; there are bars on her apartment windows, and she must fend off Bennie's unwanted attentions just as Arlie fends off the guards, who search her roughly after she tries to set a fire in her prison cell.

> GUARD-EVANS: So where is it now. Got it up your pookie,
> I bet. Oh that'd be good. Doc comin' back and me with
> my fingers up your . . . (15)

In each of these instances, the stage directions indicate that she is pinned, tied to, or sitting on the bed. Clearly, her oppression is based on sex as well as social class; it is a form of "permanent inequality."

Miller writes that in any dominant/subordinate relationship, the dominant group holds "all of the open power and authority and determines the ways in which power may be acceptably used" (9). The relationship of child to parent or student to teacher is (or should be) a relationship of "temporary inequality": the goal is the subordinate's achievement of equality with the dominant. In relations of permanent inequality, some people are defined as unequal because of race, class, sex, or other characteristics ascribed at birth. Subordinates often learn indirect ways of dealing with the dominant group because "a subordinate group has to concentrate on basic survival. Accordingly, direct, honest reaction to destructive treatment is avoided. Open, self-initiated action in its own self-interest must also be avoided" (10). This is the hard lesson Arlie learned during her last prison term. Later than most women, she found that compliance brought relative freedom, as she moved from the hospital to the honors cottage and finally out of prison altogether.

As is often the case with subordinates, however, Arlene's compliance was based on repression of her true feelings and on a complete rejection of her feeling self: the "murdered" Arlie, "killed" into silence with a fork, an implement symbolic of patriarchal control of women. Arlene's real progress toward autonomous selfhood takes place in her apartment as she learns to use words, not physical actions, to describe reality and defend her place in it. When, during a prison breakout, a cab driver touched Arlie's arm, she screamed at him but, lacking confidence in speech, also grabbed his gun and accidentally shot him. In contrast, she defends herself from Bennie by naming him a rapist and by graphically describing his actions. Finally, in telling the story of Arlie's murder to Ruby, she reclaims Arlie, her feeling self, who is now "reborn" into speech.

In *Getting Out* Arlene struggles against oppressive patriarchal institutions, graphically portrayed. In *'Night, Mother* the focus is narrower, almost microcosmic. Jessie's decision is an individual one, and indeed her struggle in the play is to claim her suicide not as a reflection on her mother or as an act of self-aggrandizement, but simply as her own personal decision. In their last moments together, Jessie and Mama rehearse Mama's role at the funeral. Mama wonders what she will say was Jessie's motive, since Jessie has asked her to keep this evening "private, yours and mine." Finally Mama decides she will say, "It was something personal," and Jessie agrees, "Good. That's good, Mama" (82).

In the background, however, lurk larger societal reasons for Jessie's decision. Although she seems to keep house competently for her mother, Jessie reminds her, "You know I

couldn't work. I can't do anything. I've never been around
people my whole life except when I went to the hospital. . . .
The kind of job I could get would make me feel worse." Her
lack of marketable skills, her preference for solitude, and the
degraded and meaningless nature of most work in our society
prohibit Jessie from using work as a way of making her life
meaningful.

Women in our society are expected as well to make something of their lives through their relationships with men. But
Jessie's father, whom she loved but never understood, is now
dead. Her husband has abandoned her. Her teenage son stole
her only valuable jewelry before he disappeared. None of
these specific problems, however, has led to her decision to
end her life. Rather, she is dissatisfied with the sum of her life,
with her self. She explains to her mother that she is not her
child any more:

> I am what became of your child. . . . It's somebody I lost,
> all right, it's my own self. Who I never was. Or who I tried
> to be and never got there. . . . So, see, it doesn't much
> matter what else happens in the world or in in this house,
> even. I'm what was worth waiting for and I didn't make it.
> (76)

While Arlene is able to relocate her child self and thus to
achieve a kind of autonomy, Jessie has no sense of self and thus
no future. As Norman explained in an interview, "Jessie
thinks she cannot have any of the other things she wants from
her life, so what she will have is control, and she will have the
courage to take that control" (Gussow, "Women Playwrights,"
39). Jessie feels she can only control her life in separation from
her mother, and through death. But although she is determined to die, Jessie is also determined to help her mother
survive this blow as well as possible.

In both plays, the protagonists seek autonomy in a context
of connection with their families: Arlene for a future with her
son, Jessie for her mother's future without her. Jessie has

stocked the pantry, cleaned the closets, and has even made a list of Christmas presents for Dawson to give Mama for the next ten years. Most importantly, she strives to explain her decision to her mother in order to alleviate the guilt her mother may feel. Mama pleads, "How can I get up every day knowing you had to kill yourself to make it stop hurting and I was here all the time and I never even saw it" (73). Jessie reassures her: "I only told you . . . so you wouldn't blame yourself. . . . I didn't want you to save me. I just wanted you to know" (74).

"Knowing is the most profound kind of love, giving someone the gift of knowledge about yourself," Norman comments (Gussow, "Women Playwrights," 40). Jessie's action in the play is to give her mother this knowledge, this connection. By so doing, she frees her from guilt and responsibility. She exercises her own freedom of choice, but in a context of responsive concern for her mother. Gilligan describes the transition she has observed in women's moral development in similar terms:

> Questioning the stoicism of self-denial and replacing the illusion of innocence with an awareness of choice, they struggle to grasp the essential notion of rights, that the interests of the self can be considered legitimate. . . . Then the notion of care expands from the paralyzing injunction not to hurt others to an injunction to act responsively toward self and others and thus to sustain connection. (149)

By honestly sharing her deepest feelings with her mother, Jessie has created a mature connection with her, replacing the childish bond of merged personalities that Chodorow describes. She defines herself as a separate but loving adult, demonstrating a distinctly female autonomy in connection. Arlene, in contrast, fails to find connection with her mother, yet it is Arlene's determination to mother Joey that drives her to attempt the "straight" life. And it is her grief for her lost child self, shared with an older woman who comforts her as a mother would, that makes her whole again.

Morally, Arlie/Arlene's development parallels that observed by Gilligan in her study of women who were facing a decision about abortion. Gilligan discerned three phases: 1) an initial focus on caring for the self in order to assure survival; 2) the development of a sense of responsibility for others, manifested through self-sacrifice; and 3) a broad perspective on the interconnection between the other and the self which dissolves the tension between selfishness and responsibility, and which Gilligan calls an ethic of care (73-74). Arlie lives in the first phase, struggling for survival. Arlene begins in phase 2, having rejected the "selfish" and "hateful" self and having decided to go "straight" despite the difficulties for the sake of Joey. As Arlene awakens to the complexity and the hardship of the path she has chosen, she has to vanquish the temptation to turn to men for help: Carl offers luxurious living and easy money instead of a grimy apartment and a dishwashing job; Bennie offers paternalistic protection and financial security. Resisting both of their appeals, Arlene learns to be self-reliant without reverting to the violent self-protectiveness of Arlie. Moreover, with Ruby's help she learns to love and accept her old self as the first step toward a new life. Arlene now not only sees herself as connected with her son Joey, but with the humor, the energy, and even the rebelliousness of Arlie.

The repeated juxtaposition of Arlie and Arlene as they respond to similar situations or use similar words forces the audience to question the meaning of Arlene's reform and to mourn what has been lost in the course of her resocialization. Before Arlene herself realizes it, the audience knows that she needs Arlie if she is going to face the future as a complete woman. Contemporary women's psychology argues that women face a particular struggle in defining the boundaries of the self, in negotiating among merging, connection, and separation. If that is so, then the very structure of this play embodies that process of negotiating new boundaries for a healthier self.

But if in *Getting Out* psychic health comes from extending

the borders of the self, in *'Night, Mother* the protagonist must delineate those borders more precisely. The intensity of Jessie and Mama's interaction epitomizes the mother/daughter relationship described by Chodorow:

> A girl continues a preoedipal relationship to her mother for a long time. . . . Mothers tend to experience their daughters as more like, and continuous with, themselves. Correspondingly, girls tend to remain part of the dyadic primary mother-child relationship itself. This means that a girl continues to experience herself as involved in issues of merging and separation, and in an attachment characterized by primary identification and the fusion of identification and object choice. (166)

In *Getting Out* Norman physicalizes the self-division of the protagonist by employing two actresses to depict the temporally removed selves of Arlene and Arlie. In *'Night, Mother* the characters are literally different people, but they form so close a community that they seem nearly to be complementary sides of one female self. Throughout the play the women alternate patterns of motion and stasis, of engagement and disengagement. Jessie begins by bustling about the house, filling candy dishes and pill bottles, preparing for her imminent departure. But when she persuades her mother to make hot chocolate "the old way," the stage directions note that "JESSIE, who has been in constant motion since the beginning, now seems content to sit" while her mother cooks. When the hot chocolate is finished, Jessie resumes her activities, emptying the garbage and refilling the honey jar, taking care of her mother as her mother undoubtedly took care of Jessie in her childhood.

Mama is convinced that Jessie is still a part of her: "Everything you do has to do with me, Jessie." She believes that she is responsible for Jessie's decision to die: "It has to be something I did." Jessie recalls her own child self as "somebody who cried and got fed, and reached up and got held and kicked but didn't hurt anybody . . . and felt your hand pulling my quilt back up over me." In that preoedipal world, mother was a part of daughter, indeed, mother was the world itself. But, "that's who I started out and this is who is left," Jessie explains. "That's what this is about. It's somebody I lost, all right, it's my own self. Who I never was" (76). Jessie strives to persuade her mother that this decision "doesn't have anything to do with you" (72). By the end of the play she has succeeded. Mama admits with her last words to Jessie that she was wrong in thinking "you were mine" (89). Paradoxically, the very night that Mama achieves her greatest closeness to her daughter is the night that she must acknowledge their distinctness as adults, and the night on which she loses her forever.

In its stark, inevitable descent toward death, 'Night, Mother, more than any other play examined here, resembles tragedy. Yet its protagonist, Jessie, is by no means the tragic hero of classical drama. Without high position or unusual nobility of character, Jessie is also without the blind hubris of the classical protagonist. She sees her situation and herself with merciless clarity; thus, her decision to die. Unlike Arlie in Getting Out, who learns first to understand, but finally to love herself, Jessie pursues her death—far more relentlessly, in fact, than Oedipus or Hamlet. While one play concludes happily and the other sadly, both reach their conclusions outside the conventions of romance. While both women in 'Night, Mother have been married, and both were disappointed in love, these relationships are peripheral to the central relationship of the play: mother and daughter. Getting Out, too, presents men as obstacles (usually), or as sources of support (occasionally), but essentially as beside the point.

The two plays share, as well, a concern for silenced and overlooked female protagonists with their roots in domestic culture. These protagonists struggle within the patriarchal society to define themselves as autonomous beings who yet maintain a caring connection with others. Thus, each can rightly be termed an example of feminist drama, and of feminist drama that has achieved substantial popular success.

The commercial success of these plays suggests that femi-

nism has permeated our culture more widely than is sometimes recognized. At the same time, Norman's plays serve to
further a feminist consciousness in popular culture. These
plays would seem to overcome the division between social
effectiveness and widespread popularity that Gottner-Abendroth
bemoans. As she observes, "overcoming this division would
return to art its original public role, allowing it to emerge as
the most important social activity" (563). In *Getting Out* and
'Night, Mother, drama reassumes its social role, publicly cele-
brating the secret worlds of women.

5 • *In the Boom Boom Room*
• *Hurlyburly*

David Rabe's *In the Boom Boom Room,* produced by Joseph Papp and starring Madeleine Kahn, opened at Lincoln Center's Vivian Beaumont Theatre in 1973. Papp produced a revised version of the play with a different cast in 1974 at the New York Shakespeare Festival Public Theatre. Following Rabe's splashy appearance on the theatre scene in 1968 with two award-winning plays produced by Papp, *Boom Boom Room* received extensive media attention. *In the Boom Boom Room* depicts a go-go dancer, Chrissy, struggling against a patriarchy that suffuses every institution and every relationship she encounters. Predictably, reviewers found it less significant than Rabe's earlier works, *The Basic Training of Pavlo Hummel* and *Sticks and Bones,* both plays set during the Vietnam War, and both revolving around male protagonists.

> What the playwright has done—especially in this new and better focused version of the script—is to offer the portrait of a woman. The central fault of the play is that the woman herself, one of nature's losers, is just not very interesting. (*"In the Boom Boom Room,"* New York Times)

Rabe himself commented on the similarities he saw between the environment of war and the world of go-go bars: "There was the same sense of proximate violence and the same sense of indiscriminate behavior being acceptable" (24 Nov. 1973). And despite the play's relative lack of success, Rabe maintained, "The world of *Boom Boom Room* illuminates the real nature of the other plays" (12 May 1976).

A 1985 Off-Broadway revival of *Boom Boom Room* by the Orange Theatre Company met with less media attention but with greater critical success. The *New York Times* reviewer commented that the play "comes encumbered with a history. But viewed for the first time on its own modest terms . . . it is full of dramatic fury" (Mitgang). The question of whether the fate of a go-go dancer is worthy of serious dramatic treatment was apparently no longer relevant. Instead, the reviewer commented that the play shows its "blood" ties to Rabe's *Hurlyburly,* playing simultaneously in New York, but that *Boom Boom Room*'s characters are "much more identifiable people." In the eleven years that passed between the two productions, a play with the clearly feminist theme of a woman's struggle for autonomy against the patriarchy had become acceptable dramatic fare.

Hurlyburly opened in April 1984 at the Goodman Theatre in Chicago, moved to Off-Broadway after a month, and finally had an extended run at the Ethel Barrymore Theatre on Broadway. Set in a Hollywood Hills apartment, the play depicts a casting director, Eddie, struggling to grow beyond both the cynical misogyny of his roommate, Mickey, and the uncontrolled aggression of their friend, Phil, who dies in the last act in an apparently suicidal car crash. Directed by Mike Nichols and performed by a star-studded cast led by William Hurt and Sigourney Weaver, *Hurlyburly* was a critical as well as a popular success.

While reviewers almost unanimously greeted the play as an important, serious work, there was no unanimity in discussions of its meaning. Richard Shickel hypothesizes that Rabe's real subject is the failure of language:

> The bitterest of the many laughs Rabe provides derives
> from his recognition that the relentless articulateness of

his people is only a higher form of inarticulateness. Since
his subject is language, he is obliged to define his characters through the rhythms of their speech, and he rises
superbly to that most difficult of playwright's challenges.
(87)

John Simon maintains that "although *Hurlyburly* emerges
(unintentionally) as a play more or less about nothing, that
nothing ascends, in its better moments, to a philosophical
nothingness, which has a sorry dignity of its own" (42). Jack
Kroll feels that "we are seeing the breakdown of values
through Hollywood jive . . . a world of intelligent nervous
wrecks who've lost their moral center and, not knowing where
to turn, turn everywhere" (67). All three reviewers note the
thread of misogyny that runs through the work, yet none
seems willing to credit this as a major theme. Rabe, however,
sees the relationship of the sexes as central to *Hurlyburly*. "A
lot of people say the play is anti-woman," he commented in an
interview. "I don't think that's true. It's about the price some
guys pay to be men" ("Hollywood," 5).

Critic Frank Rich objects when *Hurlyburly* reveals "the
tough guys' previously hidden vulnerability . . . in the manner
of a John Cassavetes male menopause film." "This is a paltry,
amorphous payoff to the strong buildup," he scolds, "and it's
unaccountably larded with intimations of nuclear apocalypse."
Similarly, Simon resents what he sees as the play's becoming
concerned with "quasi-serious philosophizing," much prefer-
ring its initial statement of "philosophical nothingness." But
the play expresses a philosophy beyond the nihilism of its
characters, a feminist philosophy which encompasses men,
women, and children, as well as the environment and the
threat of nuclear war.

Hurlyburly can, in fact, be seen as a continuation of themes
raised by *Boom Boom Room,* which views the society from the
standpoint of a powerless woman trapped by the patriarchy
and reaches despairing, deterministic conclusions. Eleven
years later, *Hurlyburly* depicts a man reacting to the new

confidence of women and to the growing awareness of society's self-destructiveness with an initial defensive fury, but finally with a humility that offers a glimmer of hope.

In the Boom Boom Room concerns a go-go dancer, Chrissy, who works in Big Tom's Boom Boom Room. She has moved to a new apartment since getting this job, and acquires new acquaintances including Guy, a gay man who lives upstairs; Al and Ralphie, who follow her home from the Boom Boom Room; Eric, who has seen her dance and wants to date her; and Susan, the announcer at the go-go bar. The opening scene introduces Chrissy and her father, Harold, as a microcosm of the patriarchy. Harold enters Chrissy's apartment by breaking into it, a simple feat for him since he is a professional criminal. Chrissy is rehearsing her go-go dancing when he enters. She offers him a sandwich. He nostalgically recalls having chased Chrissy with a belt when she was a child, but she is unclear about whether it was he or one of her uncles who chased her.

In this first, brief scene, the terms of the patriarchy are defined. Chrissy's attempt to pursue independence and self-expression through dance is interrupted by her father. Harold is the criminal intruder; Chrissy is his victim. Chrissy is the provider of food; Harold is the consumer. Harold and his brothers are described as almost interchangeably inflicting violence on the child Chrissy. The associations established in this first scene recur and develop as the play continues, but do not change. Harold continues to associate his daughter with food for his consumption. He shows Chrissy a tomato plant he is planning to grow and later eat. "Givin' somethin' life gives you that right, don't you think?" (72), he asks her. Chrissy, who used to work at the A & P, carries a thermos of coffee around to offer people in hopes that this will make them like her better. Chrissy's mother, similarly, is shown buying groceries, fixing Kool-Aid, and making chocolate pudding for her husband. She tells Chrissy that the way to a man's heart is through his stomach. Unlike the women in *The Stick Wife* or in Norman's plays, these women find no escape, even in the world of domesticity. In the patriarchy Rabe describes, women are the providers of food and, by extension, food itself for men's consumption.

Chrissy's go-go dancing, which opens the play, is another image that expands into images of all women displayed and adorned for men. In the first scene, Harold spies on Chrissy while she is dancing. In later scenes, Al, Ralphie, and Eric are all attracted to her because of her dancing. Chrissy hopes to make go-go dancing a form of self-expression; she has designed her own costume and routine based on a *Playboy* bunny's, "but softer": "Makin' up routines is hard, and costumes outa your head, 'cause then your dancin' is good, 'cause it's outa us" (11). But Susan gives her dancing lessons in which she explains that dancing the "Jerk" should look like getting punched in the stomach and straightening up again. That, according to Susan, is what men like to see: women displaying themselves, "arrogant," and then knocked down, humiliated. The other go-go dancers give Chrissy advice on displaying herself to men:

> SALLY: And somethin' else, don't be learnin' only the down and dirty dances.
>
> MELISSA: Sometimes it's coyness they want—or they want us dancing coquettishly.
>
> VIKKI: Frivolous. (17)

At one point, Chrissy despairs of ever achieving the multitude of adornments that will make her attractive to men:

> I gotta be makin' some resolutions about my stupid life. I can't not bite my fingernails. I can't not do it. I can't keep 'em long and red, because I'm a person and I'm a nervous person, and I diet and diet I might as well eat a barrel of marshmallows. My voice is not sexy or appealing. I try to raise it. I try to lower it. I got a list of good things to say to a man in bed. I say stupid stuff made up outa my head. My hands are too big. My stockings bag all the time. Nothin' keeps me a man I want anyway. I mean, how'm I gonna look like that? [Seizing a glamour magazine, she thrusts

the cover, the face of a beautiful woman, at (Guy).] I can't
do it. Not ever. (47)

Later, however, she temporarily regains hope, believing that if
she wears her hair differently or perhaps buys new underwear
she can be more attractive to men.

From the first scene, in which Harold nostalgically recalls
chasing Chrissy with a belt, the violence in the play gradually
escalates. Susan describes seeing a man cut another one open
with a razor blade. Al describes leaving his second wife when
he began wanting to kill the household pets. Ralphie, Al's
lunatic sidekick, remarks in a characteristic non sequitur, "Life
is all like World War II" (26). Finally the violence emerges
onstage when Al beats Chrissy, just before the play ends. The
relationship of man as criminal/woman as victim expands from
Harold and Chrissy to all the other characters as well. The go-
go girls describe boyfriends who "hurt them a hundred times a
day." Chrissy's mother says that her father "had women sittin'
down with coat hangers all across this state," aborting themselves after affairs because he did not like to use birth control.
The go-go dancers describe their ideal, a dancer named
Jennifer whom Big Eddie used to pay two hundred dollars to
dance to "Lovin' Feelin'." Chrissy dreams of achieving this
ideal: "Gonna be so much helpless dancin' tenderness they're
just gonna all wanna wrap me up in all their money" (19). This
image combines women displaying themselves, men with the
power to "buy" women like commodities, and the added
market value of women who display the helplessness of
victims.

All the men in the play share the power associated with
Harold, the violent patriarch. Eric is anxious to have sex with
Chrissy so he will be able to dominate their relationship.
Ralphie tells Chrissy that he is in mental contact with her
father (whom he does not, in fact, know) and that this gives
him power over her. Chrissy herself finally makes the connection between her father and all men explicit. In her final scene
with Al, she calls him "Daddyo" and addresses him as if he

were her father, accusing him of having put her "in a woman he didn't love" (108), that is, of having impregnated her mother. She has made the connection between father and husband and among all men as patriarchal oppressors.

The men in the play invoke patriarchal institutions to support their oppression of women. Ralphie, while threatening Chrissy with his supposed connection to her father, also tells her that God the Father knows everything Chrissy does, and tries to force her to eat ketchup, telling her it is blood, a kind of communion he will administer as a representative of the patriarchy. Eric struggles with religion on a more sophisticated level, arguing at first that "Mother Church" is a castrating force, but finally deciding to have sex with Chrissy and then go to confession: "I'll whisper of your power. . . . And [the priest] will tell the prayers of penance that will cleanse me of all dark cruel longing, the mystery of you" (36). The patriarchal power of the church will cleanse Eric of the imagined power of female sexuality.

Like the church, hospitals and prisons are male preserves. Chrissy asks Al and Ralphie to tell about their prison stay, since all her male relatives have been to prison and she has not. She considers seeking help from the medical institution by undergoing psychiatric counseling. But she tells Susan she could never go to a woman counselor, while Susan warns her against male counselors, saying that the word is a pun: "therapist" equals "the rapist." All institutions are controlled by men, closed to women or a threat to them.

Two characters—Susan and Guy—seem initially to have escaped the patriarchal structure. Guy, who is gay, feels an immediate kinship with Chrissy because both have been exploited by men. He suggests to her that they each seek men for sex, "And we'll come back here to tell one another of their stupidity—their peculiarity. All affection, all tender feeling will be reserved for us" (49). Unfortunately, Guy and Chrissy also share a need to be attractive commodities to men. Both of them dream of being a *Playboy* centerfold, "posed on fur." As a result, their friendship quickly degenerates into bitter rivalry. Guy is still a part of the hierarchy, although in a female role, and because he is, he cannot perceive Chrissy as other than a sexual rival.

Similarly, Susan seems at first to represent an exception to the passive females in the play. Susan says that when her high school boyfriend jilted her, she took violent revenge:

> I shot him. I didn't know you could be shot and not die, so I didn't shoot him any more. I just walked away. He lived and went on to play Big Ten football after a year delay. It's somethin', though, how once you shoot a man, they're none of them the same any more, and you know how easy, if you got a gun, they fall down. (31)

Susan has learned from this experience to be the aggressor instead of the victim. She is free to step outside the passive female role to offer Chrissy a sexual proposition. But when Chrissy seeks Susan's help in the middle of the night, Susan is unwilling to leave her male lover to help her. Like Guy, Susan offers only a reversal of the usual gender roles, not a real alternative. As Chrissy observes, Susan's behavior makes her a "man in disguise," capable of violence but incapable of tenderness. Because Susan understands how to use violence for her own ends, she has gained a more privileged position in the hierarchy—she is Big Tom's mouthpiece in the Boom Boom Room.

Big Tom is the discotheque owner, the unseen patriarch who operates not only the Boom Boom Room where women dance for men, but the Room Thomasita where men dance for men; and the Tom-Tom Room where women dance for women. Susan describes Big Tom making the rounds of his bars each night "like a man through a single home, making sure the jukebox songs are current, the customers grinning, the hookers polite and busy" (58). Just as the society of the play allows some exceptions in the gender of those who exploit and those who are exploited, Big Tom caters to all sexual tastes while retaining the power to dominate the entire system. Big Tom's discotheque is symbolic of the patriarchal society, and the title of the play tells us that all the action occurs "In the Boom Boom Room."

Boom Boom Room falls into a pattern of Chrissy's encountering each of the other characters one by one. Each character attempts to impose a limiting sexual role on Chrissy, a process she resists more and more intensely as the play progresses. In the first act, Chrissy is as yet unaware of the deterministic nature of her environment. Harold, representative of the patriarchy, tells her, "I'm a permanent fixture" (4). But Chrissy is optimistic: "I'll just keep after some things I can maybe get is sort of all I'm saying" (3). In the next scenes, she meets a series of exploitive males, but shows irritation only with Eric who has failed to compliment her new dress. She advises him:

> when you are trying to be with a person who has dances in her head all the time, and who is a special kind of person—I mean, I have dreamed of ballet all my life and other kinds of dancing-so-you-tell-a-story! Of which go-go is just a poor facsimile—and that kind of person must be treated very specially, or they will get upset with you as I just did, and maybe even yell at you. (16)

Chrissy asserts herself here for the first time, but her assertion is based on her special needs as a dancer, not on her right as a human being to decent treatment. With Al, Chrissy asserts herself only to the extent of insisting on birth control because "I was nearly an abortion in my mother, so I don't wanna ever have one on anybody else!" Act 1 ends with Chrissy responding lovingly to Al's definition of her in purely sexual terms, "You're the best lay I ever had in a long time" (37).

Act 2 begins with a soliloquy by Chrissy: "I had this lemonade stand . . . at one point in my life. An' I wanted to have a paper route, but only boys were allowed" (39-40). She is beginning dimly to perceive the general oppression of women, and this perception grows throughout act 2. In the second scene, she rejects Guy's offer to pass her off as a man,

"Christopher," at the next gay ball. "I ain't no Christopher, Guy" (55), she tells him, making her first mild claim to pride in her female identity.

Expressions of Chrissy's anger, indirect at first, begin to surface in this act. She tells Susan that she picked up a soldier in New York, led him on, and then dropped him. She admits to having spit in the shoe of one of the go-go girls of whose boyfriend she is jealous. In the last scene of this act, she attempts to confront her mother for having tried to abort her. When Chrissy's mother responds that it was her father's fault for refusing to use birth control, Chrissy flees, saying that she never wants to see either of her parents again.

In act 3 Chrissy, always approached by others, finally begins to seek people out for help: Eric, Susan, and then her parents. When Eric will not help her, she becomes genuinely angry at him, warning him that he is "messing with the universe." When she seeks Susan late at night and finds her with a man, Chrissy shoves her away, her first act of physical violence. She goes to her parents with nightmares in which she does not know if she is a man or a woman, and asks if her early memories of being sexually molested are true. Her parents say no, "All that's just something you always wanted, but not a soul ever did it to you" (91). Momentarily defeated, Chrissy decides to marry Al because "I have come to understand at last how I have lived my life so far stupid, and people'll never be happy livin' the way I have. I mean, cruel and mean and selfish. When I didn't even have a self in me. No . . . real self. But I have other virtues" (97).

Chrissy has already learned too much about her low status for her attempt at a selfless marriage to succeed. In the next scene, Chrissy's anger returns, finally directed toward Al as representative of the patriarchy. "I ain't listenin' to you any more, Daddyo! Don't you know how I ain't listenin'? I am a free person—a free goddamn person" (107). She has made the connection among all men as oppressors in the hierarchy, and among all women as oppressed. When Al curses a telephone operator, Chrissy asks, "How come you gotta call her a

bitch? . . . That's all women are to you, ain't it?" (100). She
even makes the connection between women and food as items
of consumption for men, when she tells Al, "I ain't just a hunk
of liver for you to pound on!" (101). But she will be punished
for proclaiming her autonomy in defiance of the patriarchy.
The scene ends with Al beating her brutally.

Chrissy has understood the hierarchy, but she cannot change
it. It is, as Harold warned her, "a permanent fixture." In the
last scene, Chrissy reappears making her debut in a topless
bar. The master of ceremonies—identified in the script only
as THE MAN—says that Chrissy has chosen to appear
masked and topless. "'You got your choice,' she says when I
was talkin' to her. 'What's it gonna be, face or boobies?'
'Boobies,' we told her. 'Boobies, boobies, boobies'" (111).
Her choice of costume demonstrates her comprehension of
her situation. She no longer dresses as a bright-eyed, harmless
"bunny" whose dancing is a form of self-expression. Instead,
she is costumed as a faceless sexual object. THE MAN tells
the audience that "she's been workin' hard all her life to get
this just right" (111). What Chrissy has finally gotten "right" is
her place in the immovable patriarchy. Chrissy has attempted
to assert her freedom, her existence as a full person and not
"just a hunk of liver," and she has been violently corrected,
sacrificed to the existing order.

Rabe said in a 1973 interview that writing the play was a
personal attempt to empathize with the situation of women. "I
know that the basic thing I was trying to do was very personal
and in terms of solving a distance between myself and women"
(22). Chrissy's progression from living to please others toward an attempt to define herself autonomously is in fact
characteristic of female moral development as described by
Gilligan.

> In women's development, the absolute of care, defined
> initially as not hurting others, becomes complicated
> through a recognition of the need for personal integrity.
> This recognition gives rise to the claim for equality

embodied in the concept of rights, which changes the understanding of relationships and transforms the definition of care. (166)

But at the moment that Chrissy claims her right to personal integrity, she is struck down by the patriarchy which insists on her role as passive victim.

Interestingly, Rabe's attempt to think as a woman resulted nevertheless in a play with a traditionally "male" dramatic structure. Chrissy, the isolated protagonist, struggles against a hostile society. She is, in Burke's terms, the victim sacrificed for the sake of the new, perfected order. There is no implication in the play itself, however, of either personal or societal transformation. Unlike Jessie in *'Night, Mother,* Chrissy does not choose her fate. Instead, rather like *The Brothers'* Danielle, Chrissy progresses from innocence to an almost tragic insight, but without any suggestion that she or the larger society will benefit from her hard-won knowledge.

In the Boom Boom Room, in its depiction of a monolithic patriarchy engaged in the systematic oppression of women, reflects the radical feminist thinking of its time almost perfectly. It is ironic to note this in a play which would certainly have been dismissed by most radical feminists at that time because it was written by a man. Eleven years later, Rabe again attacked relations between the sexes, this time from a male perspective that he has admitted reflects his own conflicts and those of his friends. In the intervening time, feminism has expanded its vision as well, so that in 1981, radical feminist Robin Morgan was writing that "feminism is a vision as important and transformative to men as to women, and one crucial to the continuation of sentient life on this planet" (xiii). Morgan describes the new cultural feminism as a holograph, a three-dimensional phenomenon with many aspects.

One integral aspect is, to be sure, the worldwide condition of women. Another is involved in finding the right technological balance for a new society. . . . Another exposes the complexity of sexual passion in both women and men. . . . What have been perceived as separate subjects—gender, race, global politics, family structures, economics, the environment, childhood, aging—all reveal their interconnectedness as we move around the holograph, peer underneath it, and lean above it. The internal workings of the human body, the internal workings of an atomic particle, the issues of dying and death . . . of spiritual faith and scientific fact . . . disclose themselves as interwoven expressions of one dynamic whole. (xiv)

This is the underlying philosophy of Rabe's most recent play, *Hurlyburly*.

Hurlyburly is set in the Hollywood Hills home of two casting agents, Eddie and Mickey. Phil, an unemployed actor, seeks Eddie out for sympathy on his disintegrating marriage and advice on his foundering career. Artie, a middle-aged screenwriter, brings Donna, a homeless teenage hitchhiker, to stay with Eddie and Mickey. Eddie and Mickey, meanwhile, are competing for the interest of Darlene, a photographer. Eddie suggests that he and Phil have sex with Donna, excluding Mickey to punish him for Darlene's apparent preference for him. When Phil later abuses Donna for claiming to understand football, she moves out again. Mickey finally disclaims any interest in Darlene, and she turns to Eddie as act 1 ends.

A year later, Phil, now a father but on the verge of divorce, asks Eddie and then Artie for help in understanding his destiny. The men decide that Phil needs a date, and Eddie calls a bubble dancer named Bonnie. Bonnie and Phil leave together in her car but she quickly returns, having been thrown out of the moving car by Phil. Phil disappears briefly and returns with his infant daughter, whom he has surreptitiously carried out of the house while her mother is napping.

In the first scene of act 3, several days later, Eddie finds Mickey flirting with Darlene. After Mickey leaves, this precipitates an argument that ends abruptly with a phone call announcing Phil's death in a car crash. The final scene of the play takes place after Phil's funeral. Eddie finds a note from Phil, mailed on the day of his death, reading "The guy who dies in an accident understands the nature of destiny." Unable to decipher the note's meaning or to persuade Mickey that it has significance, Eddie drives Mickey away and is ranting drunkenly at the television when Donna arrives at the door, once again seeking shelter. The play ends on a rare peaceful note, with Donna asleep on Eddie's lap.

Hurlyburly, chosen as the title after the play was in rehearsal, refers to the opening lines of the witches in *Macbeth:* "When shall we three meet again? In thunder, lightning, or in rain? When the hurlyburly's done, when the battle's lost and won." There are no direct parallels of plot or character between the two plays. Yet both *Macbeth* and *Hurlyburly* concern themselves with men confronting their own darkest nature, and with the working out of destiny in an atmosphere of "fog and filthy air." Certainly the conclusion of *Hurlyburly* is a paradoxical one, in which Eddie has both "lost and won."

The opening scene of *Hurlyburly* finds Eddie asleep in front of the television. Phil enters, asking "Eddie, you awake or not?" (2). Phil goes on to describe his latest argument with his wife. When Phil mentions that his wife is angry at Eddie as well as Phil, Eddie is dumbfounded: "I mean that's sad. She's sad. They're all sad. They're all fucking crazy. What is she thinking about? . . . None of them think. I don't know what they do" (7).

The attitude of hostile confusion toward women that Phil and Eddie display in the opening scene is characteristic of all the men in the play. Indeed, all the characters seem to live in the warlike confusion, the hurlyburly that the title suggests. Characters drift in and out without motive. Their speech is studded with nonsense words like "blah-blah-blah," "rapateta," "whatchamacallit," and "thingamajig," which the playwright says in the stage directions are "used by the characters to keep themselves talking, and should be said with the authority and conviction with which one would have in fact said the missing word" (1-2). Eddie and Mickey, seemingly the most self-

assured characters, also use nonsense words the most, usually
while attempting to defend a specious line of reasoning.
Eddie, even when he uses no nonsense words, seems to
promote misunderstandings, often as a form of self defense:

> MICKEY: What kind of tone is that?
>
> EDDIE: What do you mean, what kind of tone is that?
> That's my tone.
>
> MICKEY: So what does it mean?
>
> EDDIE: My tone? What does my tone mean? I don't have
> to interpret my fucking tone to you, Mickey. I don't
> know what it means. What do you think it means? (22)

Furthering the confusion, drugs and alcohol are used constantly by everyone in the play. But unlike many older realistic
plays in which alcohol functions as a kind of truth serum,
Hurlyburly depicts drug and alcohol use as an escape, what
Eddie describes as "the American Dream of oblivion" (95),
and as an excuse for immoral behavior. When Phil relates that
he struck his wife in the midst of their argument, Eddie
responds: "What was it? You were ripped?" (10). Later,
Mickey and Eddie relate the joke they played with Bonnie's
help on Robbie Rattigan, a television star arriving in L.A. for
an audition. Mickey and Eddie arrived at the airport with
Bonnie in the backseat of their car. Bonnie had been instruct-
ed ahead of time to "relax" Rattigan by performing fellatio on
him during the drive back. As the men are gleefully recalling
Rattigan's reaction, they suddenly remember that Bonnie's
little daughter had also been in the car, and the story begins to
sour:

> MICKEY: This is sick, isn't it? I'm gettin' a little sick.
>
> EDDIE: We were ripped though, weren't we? We were
> ripped.
>
> MICKEY: Maybe we were blotto. (91)

Immediately, they turn to drugs as an excuse for their behavior, but this time Eddie questions the validity of the excuse. "Then we woulda forgot the whole thing. Which we didn't." Finally the men agree that Bonnie was responsible, since "no one forced her" to bring her child, but Eddie points out that she cannot be blamed either:

> Once it was a guy from TV, what chance did she have? She couldn't help herself. . . . I mean, what does she watch? About a million hours of TV a week, so the airwaves are all mixed with the TV waves and then the whole thing is scrambled in her brain waves so, you know, her head is just full of this static, this fog of TV thoughts, to which she refers for everything. (93)

Television is an essential element in the hurlyburly of the play, used as a source of continuous but questionable information and therefore of further confusion. For Eddie, Artie, Mickey, and Phil, television is a source of employment as well. Nevertheless, Eddie describes TV as an actively corrupting force. In an attempt to encourage Phil in his search for employment, Eddie describes the television industry:

> Look, you have to exploit your marketable human qualities, that's all. . . . So like every other whore in this town, myself included, you have to learn to lend your little dab of whatever truth you can scrounge up in yourself to this total, this systematic sham. (20)

Eddie has revealed to Darlene that he was raised by fanatically religious parents who beat him for watching television. Although he now rejects his parents' behavior as "insane," and even uses his upbringing as another excuse for his behavior, he seems to have retained his parents' view of television as a tool of Satan, the Prince of Lies. Television's falsity seems to Eddie an appropriate metaphor for the falsity of his life. In defending his behavior to Bonnie, he tells her: "You know, we're all just background in one another's life. Cardboard cut-outs bumping around in this vague, you know, hurlyburly, this spin-off of what was once prime time life" (115).

A fog of confusion seems to the men to separate them from the women in the play. Phil tries to explain what led him to strike his wife: "Right in front of me was like this cloud with her face on it, but it wasn't just her, but this cloud saying all these mean things about my ideas and everything about me, so I was like shit and this cloud knew it" (10). Eddie, jealous of Darlene's interest in Mickey, accuses her of being indiscriminate: "I evidently have to break through this goddamn cloud in which you are obviously enveloped in which everything is just this blur totally void of the most rudimentary sort of distinction" (139). The men seem to be honestly confused by the women, but at the same time willing to remain confused rather than find out what the women are really thinking. The orderly patriarchy in *Boom Boom Room* has been replaced by a state of guerrilla warfare in *Hurlyburly*.

Unlike *Boom Boom Room,* however, in which Rabe adopted Chrissy's female viewpoint, in *Hurlyburly* his primary focus is on the men and specifically on the triangle formed by Eddie, Mickey, and Phil. Rabe says that *Hurlyburly*'s first working title was "the guys' play" ("Hollywood," 1). At the beginning of the play, Mickey and Eddie, roommates and co-workers, are united by an attitude of sophisticated cynicism. Eddie is drawn, however, to Phil's emotionality and aggression. Phil's suicidal unhappiness stems from his awareness that he is, as he says, "a merciless, totally out of control prick" (75). But Eddie delights in Phil's uncontrolled behavior, listening gleefully while Phil describes hitting his wife or getting into a fight with a stranger in a bar. When Phil expresses regret, Eddie encourages him to excuse himself: "Give yourself a break. I mean, the real issues are not you hitting people or not hitting people. . . . You enjoy hitting people and you know it" (78). Eddie, in fact, enjoys Phil's violence as much as Phil does, while at the same time defining himself as completely controlled and rational, as Phil's opposite.

Eddie's behavior in the early scenes of the play is hostile, as in his relationship with his ex-wife; competitive, as in his struggle with Mickey over Darlene; and exploitive, as in his near rape of Donna. But his hostility is hidden, seemingly even from himself, behind a barrage of sophisticated rationalizations. Finally in act 2, Eddie actively colludes with Phil's violence toward women by arranging his "blind date" with Bonnie. When Bonnie returns to upbraid Eddie, the stage directions say that Eddie reacts "increasingly as a little boy" (111). He first attempts to blame Bonnie for Phil's attack on her, then tells Bonnie and Phil he is equally disgusted with both of them. He tries to distance himself further from Phil, describing his earlier encouragement as "hype."

Eddie attempts to rationalize his increasing depression by clinging to the realm of fact and objectivity, attributing his mood first to the news in general, and then to the development of the neutron bomb. Because this bomb kills people but leaves buildings and other objects undisturbed, Eddie attributes to the bomb "this fucking *attitude* about what is worthwhile in the world and what is worth preserving. And do you know what this fastidious prick has at the top of its hierarchy— what sits at the pinnacle? *Things!*" (121). The lesson, he concludes, is "be a thing. I will be a thing and loved; a thing and live. Be harder, colder, a rock or polyurethane, that's my advice" (122).

The women in the play reproach Eddie for rationalizing his unfeeling behavior. Bonnie responds to his tirade on the neutron bomb by commenting, "Yeah, well, Eddie, it's no reason to be mean to your friends" (12). Darlene, as she is breaking off their relationship, tells him, "I don't think there's a lot more we ought to, with any, you know, honesty, allow ourselves in the way of bullshit about our backgrounds to exonerate what is our just plain mean behavior to one another" (142).

Not until the arrival of Phil's suicide note, however, is Eddie's cynical facade finally shattered. The note, mailed on the day of Phil's death, reads, "The guy who dies in an accident understands the nature of destiny. Phil" (147). Eddie attempts to comprehend the meaning of Phil's death by cracking the "code" of the note. He looks up the definitions of the note's key words in the dictionary and concludes, "So, if you die in a happening that is not expected, foreseen or intended, you understand the inevitable or necessary succession of events" (151). When Mickey resists Eddie's attempts to make sense of this, Eddie reproaches his cynicism, claiming to have loved Phil. Left alone, Eddie begins washing pills down with vodka, and tells the TV set blaring the Johnny Carson Show, "I've been humbled, John. I been blasted. . . . You never listen to me!" (161). Drugs and television no longer offer Eddie an adequate substitute for human relationships. Phil's death has shaken Eddie by its reminder of the self-loathing that lay beneath Phil's aggression, an aggression Eddie had admired. The suicide note has suggested to Eddie the hopelessness of his efforts to control his own existence in the face of a larger destiny.

It is at this moment that Donna, the child-woman, arrives. Throughout the play, references to children have formed a second cluster of images in opposition to the amoral fog of drugs, TV, and cynical verbiage. It is the presence of Bonnie's little daughter that made her behavior with Robbie Rattigan unacceptable to Eddie and Mickey. Eddie defends Phil by saying he is haunted by his unmet responsibility to his baby and to two children by a previous marriage. Children repre-sent moral responsibility to the men, but it is a responsibility they seem unable to shoulder. In the subtly chilling scene that ends act 2, the men respond to Phil's baby with tender feeling but conflate this almost at once with hatred for their ex-wives and for women in general.

Apart from Phil's baby, briefly and surreptitiously taken from her mother's home, fifteen-year-old Donna is the only real child these men confront. Her first experience with them was a series of sexual exploitations; nevertheless she has returned with the words, "Hey, Eddie! I ain't mad anymore. You mad?" Eddie admits to her, "I'm a wreck," his first confession of personal weakness in the play, and adds, "I don't know what I'm doing, you know what I mean?" Donna responds, "You're watchin' TV" (161). Although Donna's simplicity is so complete that it's funny, Eddie seems to be listening seriously to her. "But I mean, I don't know what pertains to me and what doesn't," he confesses, drawing from her the cheerfully fatalistic philosophy she espouses: "It's all part of the flow of which we are a part, too, and everything pertains to everything one way or another, see what I mean?" Eddie asks how he should respond to this "flow," and she answers, "You have total, utter, complete freedom on that score, Eddie, because it doesn't make a bit of difference" (162).

Donna, the silenced sexual object of act 1, has been revealed as a source of wisdom evocative of contemporary feminism. Donna's image of the universe as "flow" is described by Robin Morgan as the New Physics, which she employs as the central metaphor for the new feminism:

> The New Physics has taught us that space itself is indissoluble from time—that space/time is one. . . . Furthermore, we now glimpse that "mass" doesn't exist per se; mass is merely a form of energy. . . . The New Physics has moved into the realm of philosophy and consciousness more rapidly than has politics. This is because the new physicists have begun to comprehend, beginning with the breakthroughs of quantum theory and relativity theory that nothing in the universe exists independently of anything else—that all processes are interconnected, that energy itself (which is all there is) lives IN the connections. (69-70)

Next, Donna demonstrates an ability to cut through Eddie's intellectual verbiage to the emotions he is so reluctant to reveal. She asks Eddie if Phil's funeral was sad. Eddie responds with a paragraph of description including several lines of "blah-blah-blah." When he stops, she asks again, "Was it sad?" drawing from Eddie his first expression of simple grief for Phil: "this guy from way in the back of the church would

sing, and you couldn't hear the words even, just this high,
beautiful, sad sound, this human sound, and we would all start
to cry along with him" (165). Unlike Mickey, who must
distance himself from his own feelings and from Eddie's,
Donna is able simply to listen, and thus offers Eddie the
opportunity finally to express his grief. Her willingness to
listen suggests the "reverential attention to what is not oneself, to what is other to one's order" described by Donovan as
an essential element of the feminist moral vision (182).

Finally, in an effort to distract Eddie from his grief, Donna
admits that her year of hitchhiking has not taken her across the
country as she boasted when she arrived, but only to the
nearby town of Oxnard. When Eddie says that he knows
where Oxnard is, Donna responds with "immense enthusi-
asm": "It's great when people know what each other are
talking about, right, isn't that what we been talking about?"
(166). Although it is on the most rudimentary level, Eddie has
finally communicated with another human being. He has seen
Donna's willingness to forgive, her acceptance of life, and her
ability to listen deeply and to speak simply and truthfully.
Touched and thoughtful, he tells Donna, "I'm gonna be up for
a while. . . . I don't know if I'm going to sleep ever again. I
might stay awake forever" (166). Donna offers to sleep on the
floor, but Eddie invites Donna to sleep on the couch with him.
She asks if sex will again be the price of her stay, but he tells
her it will not, and as the play ends, "He holds her" (167). The
play is thus framed by Eddie sleeping alone in the opening
moments and thoughtfully awake, guarding Donna at the end.

Eddie reflects the characteristic moral and psychological
development of men described by Gilligan. Defining themselves by their accomplishments, they remain distant in personal relationships.

> Given this distance, intimacy becomes the critical experi-
> ence that brings the self back into connection with
> others. . . . The experience of relationship brings an end
> to isolation, which otherwise hardens into indifference,

> an absence of active concern for others, though perhaps a
> willingness to respect their rights. For this reason, inti-
> macy is the transformative experience for men through
> which adolescent identity turns into the generativity of
> adult love and work. (164)

As Chrissy struggles vainly for autonomy in separation, Eddie
struggles for connection.

But if *Boom Boom Room* reflects a female moral development
and *Hurlyburly* a typically male development, *Boom Boom Room*
reflects a more traditionally male dramatic structure while
Hurlyburly breaks with that tradition. Like many recent plays
by women, *Hurlyburly*'s plot relates not a series of "dramatic"
events building to a climax, but the small and seemingly
random moments of domestic relationship. Its structure is less
linear than circular as Eddie begins and ends on the sofa in
front of the TV. Although Eddie eventually emerges as the
play's protagonist, there are no clear-cut indicators of this fact
in the size and importance of the other roles. Moreover,
Eddie's personality is in some sense represented by the triangle of Mickey, Eddie, and Phil. The play can be said in a real
sense to have the community of men as its protagonist.

Thus the play's structure as well as its content reflects the
influence of women's thinking. While the play revolves around
the problems of men, the solution to their problems lies in
hearing and responding to the women. Donna, silenced and
exploited in act 1, is heard and understood in the closing
moments of act 3, providing an optimistic conclusion to the
play. Eddie, who has already recognized the threat of nuclear
war, destruction of the ecology, and neglect of children as the
causes of his despair, now breaks through on a personal level
as well, making *Hurlyburly* a drama that strongly reflects
contemporary feminist theory.

Boom Boom Room, appearing in 1973, reflected the feminism
of the early seventies and was therefore dismissed by mainstream critics, while radical feminists may have found it
difficult to accept the notion of a feminist play written by a

man. In its revival in 1985, however, it was greeted by critics as an acceptable dramatic effort, another example of the now-familiar "autonomous woman play." In the intervening years, feminist thought had progressed beyond the extreme separatism of the seventies and became a philosophy with global implications accepted by large numbers of women and a growing group of men. While Rabe's expression of this philosophy in *Hurlyburly,* opening in 1984, mystified some critics, the play was both a critical and a popular success, demonstrating feminism's growing acceptance in American society.

6 • *Top Girls*

Caryl Churchill's play *Top Girls* opens with a feminist fantasy of the past, a dinner party for extraordinary women from history and fiction, and ends with a young girl's nightmare of the future. The dream of the past reminds us of the historical weight of women's oppression, but also of the futility of individual solutions. The child's nightmare of the future reminds us what is at stake in the contemporary feminist struggle for societal transformation.

Between these two dreams lies a realistic drama that forms a critique of Marlene, a woman executive. Alternating scenes depict life at the Top Girls Employment Agency, of which Marlene is the new director, and in a working-class family in the country eventually revealed as Marlene's sister Joyce, her adopted daughter Angie, and Angie's friend, Kit. Angie, the slow-witted, overweight daughter, runs away from home to see Marlene, who is clearly nonplussed by her presence and explains to her colleagues that Angie's "a bit thick. . . . She's not going to make it" (86). The last scene of the play, a year earlier, shows Marlene in a rare visit to Joyce's home. An argument between the sisters ranging from their own life choices to Margaret Thatcher's government (supported by Marlene, opposed by Joyce) awakens Angie, who realizes vaguely that Marlene must be her mother. In the play's final moments, Angie stumbles into the living room half-awake, crying, "Frightening. Frightening" (113).

Top Girls opened at the Royal Court Theatre in London in the fall of 1982. After a successful London run, the production

Excerpts from *Top Girls,* by Caryl Churchill, reprinted by permission of Methuen London Ltd.

was brought to the Public Theatre in New York in December 1982, and it later received another production with a New York cast. *New York Times* reviewer Frank Rich praised the play's "brave gambles" and "angry wit." His review recognized that to Marlene, "the ability to make it by male success standards is the only criterion of female worth," making her "figuratively speaking, a male oppressor." His only quarrel with the argument of the play was the "absence of the middle range—of women who achieve without imitating power-crazed men and denying their own humanity." Walter Kerr echoed Rich's objection in his *Times* column a few weeks later headed, "Are These Feminists Too Hard on Women?" He enjoyed the first scene of *Top Girls* the most, "because at this juncture no one was yet trying to put anyone else down" (3), and he questioned whether a play that shows a woman as unfeeling as Marlene is toward Angie "should be called feminist at all" (13).

Nor was Kerr alone in his discomfort at labeling *Top Girls* a feminist drama. Even the actresses in the original cast, interviewed in the *New York Times,* differed on this point. Carole Hayman, who played Angie and Dull Gret, said, "It's been called a feminist play, but I would say it is a socialist play first, and a feminist play second." Lou Wakefield, who played the waitress at the dinner party, Kit, and a Top Girls client, put it differently:

> This is a feminist play in that it's self-criticism of the women's movement. The big popular wave of the women's movement was geared toward women being success-ful and equal. What Caryl Churchill is doing is asking you to reassess what is happening to the popular women's movement, not necessarily the intellectual feminist. Some women are succeeding and getting on very well, but it's no good if feminism means that women get on and tread on men's heads, or other women's heads, as hard as men ever tread on theirs. If women do get the top jobs, there's also a job to be done in reassessing that job in feminist or humanitarian terms. (Quoted in Bennets, "Top Girls")

Churchill addresses an audience that already accepts the feminist struggle for individual autonomy and asks them to criticize its limitations as many contemporary theorists have begun to do.

Bell Hooks points out that the modern feminist movement in the United States began with Betty Friedan, who address-ed the problem of the white, middle-class housewife as if it were the problem of all women—ignoring the poor, the nonwhite, and the unmarried. The demands of these women for meaningful work with equal pay and social equality with white middle-class men were easily co-opted by the capitalist patriarchy. The underlying "ideology of domina-tion" remains untouched by these women's individual gains, however, while they themselves may assume that the feminist struggle is over, or may even join the ranks of the oppressors (*Feminist Theory*).

Jean Baker Miller asserts that "even in their traditional roles, women, by *their very existence,* confront and challenge men because they have been made *the embodiment of the dominant culture's unsolved* [psychological] *problems*" (58). In response to this threat, and as a fundamental step in the male maturation process of separation from mother, many men have denied the female in themselves. This denial has created the patriarchal culture of constant wars, imperialism, and technological destruction of the environment. Women, raised by women, have tended to remain in connection, first with their mothers and later with the larger community. Because women have traditionally experienced political oppression and assignment to the domestic sphere, they have tended to develop an alternative culture and ethic (Donovan). As other options develop for middle-class women, however, the likeli-hood that they will continue to unthinkingly adopt an alterna-tive female ethic fades. Instead, they may conclude that success in a patriarchal system demands the adoption of patriarchal values. Only by conscious moral choice can the "ethic of care" described by Gilligan be retained in a changing society (Elshtain). It is by this standard of conscious moral choice that Marlene and the other "top girls" in Churchill's play are tried and found wanting.

In the opening scene of *Top Girls,* Marlene hosts a dinner to celebrate her promotion to managing director of the Top Girls Employment Agency. The guests are all extraordinary women drawn from history, art, or literature—a group of characters who had haunted Churchill for years (Keyssar, "Churchill," 214). They include the Victorian adventurer and travel writer, Isabella Bird; Lady Nijo, a medieval concubine who became a wandering Buddhist nun; Pope Joan, who may have passed as a man to become pope for a brief period in the ninth century, and Dull Gret, who leads a charge of peasant women through hell in a Brueghel painting. In a long, chatty scene that is funny and touching by turns, these women relate their life stories.

Almost a parody of feminist glorifications of women's community—Judy Chicago's famous work of art springs to mind—the dinner party is also a serious comparative study of the lives of remarkable women, historical and fictional, a kind of dramatized Women's Studies class. Like Chicago's "Dinner Party," the women are "either historical or mythological figures . . . [chosen] for their actual accomplishments and/or their spiritual or legendary powers" (Chicago, 52). Chicago's massive tribute, entailing thirty-nine ceramic place settings on embroidered runners arranged on a triangular table, is intended quite simply as a celebration of women's heritage. While it certainly succeeds in "elucidating the glory and misery of woman's history" (Snyder, 34), the piece has been criticized as "over-explained, its ideas somewhat obvious, its form too literally tied to a predetermined, rather heavy-handed content" (Caldwell, 35).

Churchill's dinner party, in contrast, offers no explanation for the women selected, relates their lives in continually overlapping and interrupted dialogue, and presents the women with a lively irreverence that is often very funny. Isabella Bird, a courageous traveler and a best-selling author of her time, is full of hypocritical regrets and psychosomatic symptoms that provided her with excellent excuses for further travel. Lady Nijo confesses that she never enjoyed the "rough life" of a Buddhist nun. "What I enjoyed most was being the Emperor's favorite and wearing thin silk" (6).

Although their conversation is informal supper talk interrupted by food and drink orders (Pope Joan orders canelloni and a salad), they are searching for commonalities, giving the scene the intellectual cast of a Women's Studies seminar on exceptional women. "Have we all got dead lovers?" Joan asks, and only Marlene responds, "Not me, sorry" (14). In fact, despite the wildly and sometimes hilariously disparate circumstances of their lives, commonalities among the diners quickly emerge. Isabella Bird, Pope Joan, and Lady Nijo were all adventurous women who in some sense "passed" as men. All three had lovers who died, and Nijo and Joan both lost children to the patriarchy—Nijo because her children were by lovers and not by the Emperor, Joan's baby being the cause of her own discovery and death by stoning. Isabella, though briefly married, never had children, and seems to have felt affection only for her sister, whom she nevertheless seldom saw because of her extensive travels. Thus isolated from other women and from family life, they are all terrible egotists who interrupt one another continually—less a community than a group of competitors. They either browbeat or ignore the young, unnamed waitress who never speaks. Of the diners, only Dull Gret is similarly silent, eating her way through the breadbasket and the scene, revealing only in response to the others' questions that she raised ten children and a pig.

Chaucer's Patient Griselda arrives late, and seems at first to present a contrast to the other, more active women. As Marlene draws out her story, however, points of agreement begin to emerge. Like Griselda, Isabella and Nijo felt most closely identified with their fathers to whom they offered perfect obedience. Griselda was not reluctant to swear the same obedience to her husband because "I'd rather obey the Marquis than a boy from the village," she says, and Marlene responds, "Yes, that's a point" (27). When the Marquis takes her children from her one by one, Lady Nijo agrees that "of course you had to [accept it], he was your life. And were you in favour after that?" (28). Griselda's uncritical acceptance of the patriarchy ultimately elevates her to a position of the highest status, far above the peasant class into which she was born— much like Marlene.

In fact, the apparently autonomous lives of all the diners have been predicated on a patriarchal system that simply co-opted them, and at a high price in isolation and suffering. Toward the end of the scene, Marlene begins to wonder, "Oh God, why are we all so miserable?" (23). Despite their adventures, their privilege, and their visibility to history, these women are miserable because they are the lonely and power-less pawns of the patriarchy. Their similarities despite the separation of their lives by hundreds of years suggest a complete lack of historical progress. Each had great adventures; nevertheless, as Isabella Bird says in the closing lines of the scene, the adventure was "only temporary" (35).

At the end of the scene, Dull Gret finally breaks her silence, revealing herself as the true exception to the group. She begins by describing Hell, a place "like the village where I come from." She says she rallied the other women around her for her fight against the devils. They were unafraid: "Well we'd had worse, you see, we'd had the Spanish. We'd all had family killed. Men on wheels. Babies on swords. I'd had enough, I was mad, I hate the bastards" (34). Unlike the other "top girls," Gret remains a member of the lowest class and leader of her community. She identifies herself with other women, does not give up her children for her own advancement, and in fact is moved to fight not only for herself but for the children and the men as well.

Judy Chicago says that the women represented in *The Dinner Party*

> tried to make themselves heard, fought to retain their influence, attempted to implement or extend the power that was theirs, and endeavored to *do what they wanted*. They wanted to exercise the rights to which they were

entitled by virtue of their birth, their talent, their genius
and their desire but they were prohibited . . . because
they were women. (54; emphasis added)

Like the diners in Churchill's opening scene, they had purely
selfish goals. While Chicago pays lip service to the still unacknowledged "powerless peoples of the world" (56), she clearly identifies herself with those she has enshrined, who were
entitled by birth or talent to "do what they wanted." Her own
strategy for completing this massive work was to engage
numerous unpaid assistants, mostly female. Thus, while she
mourns the exploitation of silenced women in her work, she
also completes the work through women's unpaid employment, while she accepts the credit as creator. *The Dinner Party*
is a remarkable achievement, but it is also fraught with un-
voiced contradictions. Churchill pointedly intends the contradictions of her historical dinner party, and goes on in subse-
quent scenes to apply them to contemporary life.

Act 1 of *Top Girls* jumps from the dinner party in scene 1 to
Marlene interviewing a client at the Top Girls Employment
Agency in scene 2, to Angie and Kit hiding from Joyce in the
backyard in scene 3. No explanation is offered of the relationship among the scenes, and only Marlene appears in more than
one of them. Although Angie refers to an aunt whom she
suspects may be her real mother, she never mentions Marlene
by name. Thus the audience is forced to imagine their own
connections among the three scenes that comprise act 1.

These sudden shifts in scene and style, criticized by some
reviewers, can also be viewed as a deliberately jarring use of
Brechtian alienation technique. Janelle Reinelt points out that
British feminists including Churchill have often adopted
Brechtian techniques in an effort to "make ideology visible"
(154). Significantly, the stage directions offer no time, only a
place for each of the first three scenes. All three seem meant to
occur in an eternal present time. Certainly this is true of the
dinner party, in which much of the humor arises from bringing
together women from such widely varied time periods. The

dinner party also serves to "historicize" the contemporary scene that follows, making Marlene's achievement less a sign of progress. Instead, she is categorized as one of that group of anomalous women throughout history who escaped the fate of invisibility but whose lives have failed nevertheless to alter the patriarchal system.

In scene 2, Marlene's advice to her young client suggests that she not only is no reformer of the present capitalistic patriarchy, she actually helps to promulgate it. She coolly assesses twenty-year-old Jeanine on the basis of her scores at school and her "presentation" of herself, advises her not to mention marriage plans to any potential employers, and recommends a job prospect that will "grow with the concern and then you'll be in at the top with new girls coming in underneath you" (38). She teaches Jeanine, in other words, to be competitive, isolated, and totally achievement oriented—like herself and the other "top girls" at the dinner party in scene 1. When Jeanine asks wistfully about travel prospects, Marlene inquires, "Does your fiancé want to travel?" Clearly, the sacrifices Isabella Bird and Lady Nijo made for their freedom are still required to some extent today.

Scene 3, like scenes 1 and 2, presents a community of females. Although this one is the more traditionally domestic group of mother and children, the characters seem no less alienated from one another. As the scene opens, Angie and Kit are hiding from Joyce in a shelter made from junk. When Joyce stops calling to Angie and goes inside, Angie remarks, "Wish she was dead." Here a depressing alternative to the top girls' adventures is presented as Joyce nags endlessly at the sullen Angie, first to come inside, then to clean her room, while Kit and Angie struggle for money and permission to go to the cinema to see *The Exterminator*.

The two children, Kit and Angie, are as intensely close now as only adolescents can be, but it is clear that the hierarchical system will soon separate them. Already Kit, three years younger than Angie, has continued longer in school and is in a higher "track" than Angie was. Kit's dream of becoming a nuclear physicist may be possible; as she points out to Joyce, "I'm clever" (53). Angie, on the other hand, is "not going to get a job when jobs are hard to get," according to Joyce. "She'd better get married. I don't know who'd have her, mind. She's one of those girls might never leave home" (52). Although Kit is clearly the luckier of the two, her choice of career is based on her fear of nuclear war. She confides that she lies awake at night wondering whether she would be safer if she moved to New Zealand, or if she should "find out where they were going to drop it and stand right in the place" (46). Angie is less interested, but only because she is focused on fantasies of killing Joyce and running off to join her glamorous "aunt," Marlene.

It is not until act 2 that the story reenters chronological time with a long series of consecutive encounters on "a Monday morning" at the Top Girls Employment Agency. In these scenes we begin to see Marlene's adoption of patriarchal values not as exceptional, but merely as unusually thorough and successful. In one interview the Top Girls representative, Win, forces a middle-aged woman to realize that she has given her life to her company but will never receive further advancement, and now is in competition with younger, more stylish women for positions in other firms. In another, Shona, a young woman in sales, is urged to present herself as having "the guts to push through to a closing situation. They think we're too nice. They think we listen to the buyer's doubts. They think we consider his needs and his feelings." Shona assures her interviewer, Nell, that "I never consider people's feelings." Then, when urged to describe her present job, she is reduced to detailing what she would order for dinner on the road, revealing her resumé as a fraud (79). Nell responds with simple exasperation, "Christ what a waste of time" (82). Nell, like Shona, Win, and Marlene, seems without ethical concerns of any kind. All are simply the heartless representatives of the heartless business world.

At one level, then, the play is a critique of the individual woman who achieves equality in the work world without regard for her sisters (literal or figurative), and even at their expense. Marlene and her associates are not simply oppressors, however, as some reviewers suggested; they are victims of the system as well. Just as the dinner party ends in drunken mourning over the lost children, the loneliness, and the violent endings to which the diners came, so the present-day female executives feel the loss of family and friends. It is only in fantasy that Marlene could celebrate her promotion with a dinner party; in reality, she says, she fell asleep in front of the television. She sees her mother, sister, and daughter perhaps once in three years; she has never married, but has had two abortions. Win, whose very name suggests her competitive nature, describes her idea of a wonderful weekend: sneaking into her married lover's house with him while his wife is away. She admits that she has had a drinking problem, that her second husband has been in prison for three years, and that she "went bonkers for a bit, thought I was five different people" (84).

Nor is the traditional upper-middle-class couple in a better situation, as represented by Howard Kidd, who lost his anticipated promotion to Marlene. According to Mrs. Kidd, who comes into the office on this same Monday morning to confront Marlene, Howard is devastated by losing his promotion, and worse, losing it to a woman who will now be his supervisor. "It's me that bears the brunt," says Mrs. Kidd. "I'm not the one that's been promoted. He's not being dominated by me, I've been right behind him, I put him first every inch of the way. And now what do I get? You women this, you women that. It's not my fault." Marlene says she is sorry that Howard's been taking it out on Mrs. Kidd, but adds, "He really is a shit, Howard" (76), an opinion the audience is likely to share. Still, when Mrs. Kidd is called away by the news that Howard has had a heart attack, it's difficult to share the cool reaction of the women executives who point out, "Lucky he didn't get the job if that's what his health's like" (85).

Mr. and Mrs. Kidd represent the traditional dichotomy described by Miller, in which the man defines himself as isolated, autonomous, and aggressive, while the woman carries the emotional, expressive burden for both husband and wife. Thus they remind the audience, who by now have seen plenty of unlikable behavior from the "top girls" that traditional sex roles are as much a dead end as their imitations of male selfishness. "We all need *both* ourselves *and* each other. Our troubles seem to come from an attempt to divide ourselves so that we force men to center around themselves and women to center around 'the other.' From this division both groups suffer" (70). In the case of the Kidds (whose name suggests their immaturity), the same pressure to compete in a capitalistic patriarchy that drives Kidd to abuse his wife cuts him down with a heart attack and hardens the hearts of (even) his female colleagues against him. Mrs. Kidd, by staking her ego entirely on her husband, sets herself in isolated opposition to other women.

Her tirade against Marlene is witnessed by Angie, who has just "run away" to Marlene. While Angie is full of admiration for Marlene's aggressive handling of Mrs. Kidd, Marlene is clearly baffled and repelled by Angie. When Win asks about Angie, Marlene can only assess her as she would an unsuccessful Top Girls client, speculating that she will grow up to be a grocery store packer. "She's a bit thick. She's a bit funny," Marlene tells Win (86). In the final scene of the play, these closing words of scene 1 achieve their full resonance with the disclosure that Marlene is Angie's mother.

Act 2, scene 2 takes place "a year earlier. Sunday evening." Thus, while time is specific in act 2, chronology is reversed. Just as the opening scene of the play denies historical progress in the condition of women, the structure of the play itself moves from a vague, eternal present in act 1 to a regression into the past in act 2. This spiraling or circular structure, characteristic of women's writing, seems here to say that human society is "going in circles"; no progress is being made.

The roots of Marlene's present circumstances are finally revealed in this scene, while her life choices are contrasted with her sister's. Marlene's struggle as an adolescent was for a personal, isolated autonomy more typical of masculine psychological development. A working-class girl with an illegitimate child, she abandoned her daughter to be raised by her married sister and sought a career in the city. Since then, she has found opportunities to travel (she worked in America for a time) and is clearly on the "fast track" in her career. Though Marlene elicits sympathy when she describes fleeing the "dead end" life she saw their mother live with their crude, violent father, her abandonment of her daughter and her rejection of the working class, including her own family, can scarcely be construed as admirable. Marlene, whose rise to the executive suite many middle-class feminists might unthinkingly admire, is, like her ghostly dinner companions, a selfish, isolated snob.

Joyce, in contrast, still lives in the community where she grew up and supports herself and her adopted daughter by cleaning houses. She has retained strong family ties to Angie and to her own mother, whom she now visits weekly in a nursing home. She defends their father to Marlene despite his violent behavior, saying that he worked "in the fields like an animal" (109). She has maintained her self-respect by breaking off her marriage after her husband's repeated infidelities, by fending off the husbands of friends after her divorce, and by supporting herself and Angie without financial help from Marlene. If Joyce represents the more traditional female development in her commitment to family and community, she also demonstrates the powerless position in which this commitment places her.

In the play's final scene, Joyce and Marlene spell out their differences. Marlene declares she favors Margaret Thatcher's government, believes in the individual, and doesn't "believe in class. Anyone can do anything if they've got what it takes," she says (111). Of course, "If they're stupid or lazy or frightened, I'm not going to help them get a job, why should I?" she adds. In one of the play's most telling moments, Joyce responds, "What about Angie? . . . She's stupid, lazy and frightened. What about her?" (112).

Angie's "frightening" dream a few minutes later concludes

the play. Although she consciously admires Marlene, her unconscious, dreaming response tells a deeper truth. If Angie, representing those children who will never be at the "top" of any hierarchy, has only Marlene to depend upon, then she and the society have every reason to fear. Marlene has practiced denial of the female to such an extreme that she brushes off her abortions as "boring. . . . messy talk about blood" (105) and avoids visiting her mother because it makes Marlene "feel better" to stay away (104). The impact of her individualistic politics on the rest of society—even on her own family— escapes her entirely. She predicts that "the eighties are going to be stupendous" and misses the irony in Joyce's response: "Who for?" (108).

Top Girls draws on the strategies of radical feminist theatre groups of the sixties and early seventies. As in many of those productions, there is no clear protagonist in the play; while Marlene is a central figure, she is by no means the active, sympathetic protagonist of traditional drama. The cast is entirely female, and each cast member with the exception of Marlene takes on two and sometimes three roles. (The characteristic Churchill touch comes with the choices of characters to be double-cast. Pope Joan, for instance, reappears as the older executive who "passed as a man at work," she felt, but now finds herself stuck in middle management.) The final scene's debate between the two sisters typifies the direct didacticism of the early works. The centrality of women characters, the satiric commentary on contemporary women's experience in the work world, and the extended reference to heroic women of the past are all characteristic of the work of these groups (Brown; Natalle).

At the same time, the play is typical of feminist drama of the eighties in its concern with silenced women, its reflection on women's community, and its depiction of female psychological and moral development. Marlene, who keeps her illegitimate daughter and her two abortions secret, is forced to silence her female experience in order to "pass" in the patriarchal business world. The silent peasant Gret, whose sole speech forms the climax of the dinner party, foreshadows the silent Angie, whose anguished cry closes the play.

The issue of women's community is raised in the tension between an all-female cast and the lack of communal feeling that pervades the dinner party, the employment agency, and even the home. Of all the characters in the play, only Angie and Kit show any warmth for one another, and their relationship is not destined to outlast childhood. The two sisters, Joyce and Marlene, illustrate the traditional female psychological development and its contemporary variant: the attempt to deny the female and adopt masculine attitudes and behavior. Joyce's relative passivity and her commitment to her mother and her niece form a contrast with Marlene's isolation and constant quest for "adventures." Joyce makes ethical decisions based on empathic concern for those around her; Marlene feels no responsibility other than to play by the cutthroat rules of the business world. If the self-centered Marlene with her complete lack of maternal concern represents the final triumph of feminism in our society, then the future is indeed "frightening."

Clearly, *Top Girls* is directed at an audience that is both sympathetic and conversant with feminist views. The 1986 Gallup Poll showing that 56 percent of all American women identify themselves as feminist, and only 4 percent "antifeminist" (Ehrenreich), no less than the mainstream press coverage and the box office appeal of Churchill's plays, confirm the existence of such an audience. Churchill, however, does not offer this audience a comfortable reinforcement of their beliefs. Instead, she challenges them to move beyond individual solutions to confront the larger contradictions created by a capitalistic patriarchy. In fact, the play demands nothing less than a feminist transformation of society. As Jean Baker Miller writes, "It now seems clear we have arrived at a point from which we must seek a basis of faith in connection— and not only faith but recognition that it is a requirement for the existence of human beings" (88). Frank Rich misses the point when he defends women who achieve without "losing their humanity" against *Top Girls'* indictment. It is not only the individuals but the patriarchal system itself that is being indicted, and the loss of humanity is everyone's loss.

7 • The Search for Signs of Intelligent Life
   in the Universe
   • The Well of Horniness
   • Last Summer at Bluefish Cove

"Feminist criticism has generally avoided the discussion of comedy, perhaps in order to be accepted by conservative critics who found feminist theory comic in and of itself," observes Regina Barreca in *Last Laughs: Perspectives on Women and Comedy*. Yet the ranks of women writers and performers of comedy are great and rapidly swelling. Jane Wagner's *The Search for Signs of Intelligent Life in the Universe,* a virtuosic one-woman vehicle for Lily Tomlin, has been among the most commercially successful feminist dramas of the eighties. At the avant-garde end of the theatre spectrum, *The Well of Horniness* by Holly Hughes, a wildly farcical send-up of "romantic" cultural icons, has launched Hughes's career as a lesbian performance artist and award-winning playwright. Jane Chambers's *Last Summer at Bluefish Cove* falls somewhere between these two, approaching a lesbian romance with realistic seriousness, but lacing its poignant love story with gentle humor. The use of comedy and romance in each of these three plays suggests what characteristically female versions of comedy and romance might be.

The Search for Signs of Intelligent Life in the Universe has all the characteristics of feminist drama alluded to in earlier chapters. Full of jokes, it is obviously a comedy. Yet it differs in important ways from traditional comedy, as described, for

Excerpts from *The Search for Signs of Intelligent Life in the Universe,* by Jane Wagner, reprinted by permission of Harper & Row, Publishers, Inc.

example, by Northrop Frye. In Frye's taxonomy, comedies are either romantic, ending in marriage and the establishment of a new, perfected hierarchy, or they are ironic, ending fatalistically. *The Search* is antiromantic, open-ended, yet optimistic in its conclusions about society.

In its humor as well, *The Search* shows both female and feminist qualities. Beginning at least as far back as Freud and continuing to the present, psychologists have defined the display of aggressive wit as a male activity. As in other areas of psychology, women, who tend to engage in self-deprecating humor instead, have been compared to this male norm and found wanting. I would propose, instead, the possibility of a positive, female value in self-deprecating humor. Feminist critics have observed in women's comic writing a tendency to mock social institutions rather than individuals, using irony as a tool against the patriarchy. This, too, is true of *The Search,* as well as of the other two plays considered in this chapter.

The Search for Signs of Intelligent Life in the Universe was performed as a work in progress in several cities around the country before opening at the Plymouth Theatre on Broadway in 1986 for an extended run. A documentary was produced for public television on its making, and the play was published by Harper and Row. Marilyn French notes in the afterword to that volume that a worldwide tour of the play is planned, as well as a cable television production. French hails the play as "the first work I know of that simply takes it as a given that a mass audience will accept feminist attitudes, that proceeds on the assumption these attitudes are shared and that therefore does not lecture, hector or even underline" (222). As such, she believes the play has societal significance: "Don't tell me feminism is dead! It's alive and well and living at the Plymouth Theatre, Broadway, New York (and in San Diego, Los Angeles, Seattle, Portland, Houston, Lexington, Atlanta, Aspen and Boston—all places where Tomlin performed and Wagner revised this show as a work in progress)" (223). Chinoy and Jenkins, writing in *Women in American Theatre,* disagree with French about the play's significance, calling it

"an anomaly—an award-winning feminist piece in the heart of
the traditional commercial theatre district. The achievement is
explained, perhaps, as much by its nonconfrontational style as
by the talents of its creators" (276). *The Search* is undeniably a
comedy, but this need not reduce its impact on an audience
nor its cultural significance. It is, in fact, structurally, psychologically,
and politically an almost perfect expression of contemporary
feminism presented in a commercial, comedic form.

   The Search opens with Tomlin's portrayal of Trudi, an
insane bag lady who demands that the audience, "*Look* at me
. . . I'm not just talking to myself. I'm talking to you, too" (13).
Trudi goes on to assert that her insanity is intentional: "I
refuse to be intimidated by reality anymore. After all, what is
reality anyway? Nothin' but a collective hunch . . . reality was
once a primitive method of crowd control that got out of
hand" (18). Thus in the opening moments of the play a bag
lady, certainly a marginal member of society, demands the
attention of a Broadway audience, points out the relative
nature of the patriarchal society's perception of what is "real"
and important, and even suggests the coercive nature of this
perception. The play's many other characters include two
prostitutes, a child, and at least three lesbians, one of them
black. Thus the play functions as a feminist drama at the most
basic level by bringing silenced, marginalized women to
speech.

   Trudi goes on to explain that she is in communication with
extraterrestrials and that she receives mental flashes of other
people's lives. "Not only do I have a linkup to extraterrestrial
channels, I also got a hookup with humanity as a whole.
Animals and plants too. . . . It's like somebody's using my
brain to dial-switch through humanity" (21-23). This "dial-
switching" creates the structure of the play, which alternates
between scenes from the lives of all the people who flash
through Trudi's brain, and Trudi herself, who shares her own
observations on the nature of humanity and those of her
extraterrestrial friends directly with the audience. Tomlin
makes the transitions among all these characters without

exiting or even making costume changes, simply by turning her back momentarily to the audience. Her sole technical support is an elaborate sound track providing appropriate background noises for the different scenes. The characters appear initially to be related only by their appearances in Trudi's psyche, but as the play develops, circumstantial connections between the characters are revealed as well.

Agnus Angst, for instance, is the fifteen-year-old daughter of Janet, the avant-garde lesbian performance artist who was briefly the lover of Lyn, a divorced feminist rereading her journal of the seventies, and the granddaughter of Lud and Marie, who take Agnus in when her father kicks her out. Lyn and Edie are members of the same consciousness-raising group as Marge, who finds the narcissistic sperm donor, Paul, to father Edie's lover's baby. Chrissy, who appears at Paul's health club complaining of her lack of job skills and confessing to having once considered suicide, reappears briefly as Lyn's incompetent secretary, and more significantly as the probable author of a suicide note found by the bored, wealthy Kate. The characters themselves are unaware of many of these links, but in the final scene, Kate meets and shares a joke with Trudi and her two friends, prostitutes who had been the subject of an earlier scene. This meeting occurs outside Carnegie Hall after a performance by child violinists, among them Ivan, the child created by artificial insemination and raised by the lesbian couple.

Although *The Search* is a one-woman show, it exemplifies both the merged ego boundaries that Chodorow describes as typical of female psychology and the communal nature of feminist drama itself, beginning with the process of its creation. While Jane Wagner is credited as sole author of *The Search,* the show developed as a collaboration between Tomlin and Wagner, the latest in a personal and professional relationship of fifteen years' standing. As Wagner describes their collaborative process, "There's always a give-and-take, and there's a chemistry that comes from this that makes you both re-examine where you are; in arguing, the input creates another perspective from the ones either of you started with" (Bennets, "Behind Lily Tomlin, Another Star"). Another interviewer noted that, "when Miss Tomlin speaks about her work, it is always in the plural—WE are striving for something different, WE are getting better mail, WE are excited about Broadway" (Fein, 4). The other half of this "we," Fein notes, is Jane Wagner. While each woman is a highly creative individual in her own right, their own sense of themselves is clearly in connection with one another.

An audience witnessing *The Search* may or may not be aware of this link between Wagner and Tomlin, but it is unavoidably reminded of at least one connection among the characters: all are performed by Tomlin. Just as in *For Colored Girls,* the portrayal of several characters by one performer points up not only the versatility of the performer but the human bond linking the characters. The large number of diverse characters, ranging from children to the elderly and including two male characters among the numerous females, reinforces the play's communal theme very strongly, despite the cast of one.

Within the play itself, Trudi performs the same function as Tomlin: she unites all the characters in her "dial-switching" through humanity. Among these characters is "this dark-haired actress / on a Broadway stage. I know her. I see her all the time outside / the Plymouth Theatre, Forty-fifth Street." In the published script, this character's name is Lily, and Lily as herself delivers short monologues typical of stand-up comedy in style. Again, as in *For Colored Girls,* we are presented with a complex series of relationships mirrored by character, performer, and creator, rather like the picture Trudi describes on a cereal box: "You know how on the front is a picture of that guy holding up a box of Cream of Wheat / and on *that* box is a picture of that guy holding up a box of Cream of Wheat / and on *that* box is a picture of that guy holding up a box of Cream of Wheat" (29), which her extraterrestrial friends see as "a picture of infinity."

Trudi's ability to "dial-switch" to the lives of all the other characters also represents a logical extreme of female psychology, an ego totally permeated by the lives of others. Trudi suggests that her madness is not entirely negative, and was, in some sense, chosen: "I got the kind of madness Socrates talked about, 'A divine release of the soul from the yoke of custom and convention.' I refuse to be intimidated by reality anymore'" (18). This notion that what appears to be insanity is simply a different perspective, while presented in comically hyperbolic terms, suggests the work of Gilligan and Chodorow. Their attempt is to deconstruct the belief that women's psychology is abnormal because it differs from the normative male model. Gilligan observes that "when women do not conform to the standards of psychological expectation, the conclusion has generally been that something is wrong with the women" (14). Among the "faults" of women identified by psychological theorists from Freud to Piaget to Erikson are a reluctance to succeed at the expense of others, a sensitivity to the perceived needs of others, and an assumption of responsibility for the care of those around them. The notion that these are faults suggests to Gilligan "a conception of adulthood that is itself out of balance, favoring the separateness of the individual self over connection to others, and leaning more toward an autonomous life of work than toward the interdependence of love and care" (17).

Trudi, of course, has resolved the problem of maintaining a balance between autonomy and connection in a rather extreme way: she has simply "dropped out" of reality into a madness that is all connections. For other characters in the play, however, finding this balance poses a primary dilemma. Paul, the sperm donor, has "lost track" of his ex-wife and his son by her, and is haunted by the notion that he may have a "secret kid" from whom he will always be equally distant. Yet at the same time, he is unable to form a close bond with anyone: "when I sense some girl digging me, / I don't get so turned on; instead, I get this / trapped feeling" (48). Having valued the "separateness of the individual self over connection to others," he is now left feeling "burnt out" and empty, but unable to change. Kate, similarly, carries around a magazine

article, "Rich People's Burn-Out," which argues that she and
her sophisticated friends are in danger of being literally bored
to death. Lily the actress says in one of the first scenes, "I
worry no matter how cynical you become, it's never enough to
keep up. I worry where tonight fits in the Cosmic Scheme of
things. I worry there IS no Cosmic Scheme to things" (26).
Agnus Angst, the teenage daughter of two work-absorbed
parents, represents a problematic consequence of this dilemma. Suffering from the neglect of both her scientist father and
her performance-artist mother, she has developed into a
lonely and nihilistic teenager with "the manners of a terrorist"
(82).

All these people represent a view opposing Trudi's, who, of
course, is very much in touch with the Cosmic Scheme, and
believes her "unique hookup with humanity could be evolu-
tion's awkward attempt to jump-start itself again" (115). Nor
is Trudi alone in her belief that connection represents humanity's salvation. In a humbler way, Lud and Marie stand for the
same impulse to connect when they take Agnus into their
home and try to win her over by making "little chocolate milk
mustaches" the way they did when she was five. Brandy, one
of the prostitutes, tells how she put a stranger, a young gay
man named Bucci, through beauty school, simply to keep him
from a life of prostitution she felt he could not survive. Even
the snobbish Kate finally connects, when she finds Chrissy's
suicide note and realizes "just how closed off I've been to
people's suffering, even my own" (210).

Throughout the play, Trudi has emphasized the arts as one
of the few achievements of humanity she can present proudly
to the extraterrestrials. They are mystified at first by her
attempts to distinguish between a can of soup and a Warhol
painting of the can of soup: "This is soup. This is art," she
keeps drilling them. But when she takes them to a play, they
experience goose bumps, not at the performance onstage, but
at their observations of the audience. "They said, 'Trudy, the
play was soup . . . the audience . . . art" (212). In other words,
the audience, "a group of strangers sitting together in the dark,

laughing and crying about the same things," has formed a community of disparate people that mirrors the one onstage. When they go out onto the street, they may, like the characters outside Carnegie Hall, see one another more clearly and perceive their own links with the rest of humanity as Trudi does hers.

Thus, *The Search,* like other plays examined here, notably *Hurlyburly,* is expressive of the feminist ethic described by Robin Morgan as the New Physics. The theory Morgan describes, that "nothing in the universe exists independently of anything else—that all processes are interconnected, that energy itself (which is all there is) lives IN the connections" (70), is one that Wagner employed quite consciously in the creation of *The Search.* "What I really started with was the quantum inseparability principle," Wagner explained in a *New York Times* interview. "I had started to read science, and to realize that physicists today are saying what metaphysicists said 2,000 years ago. We're all connected; we all time-share the same atoms and the same time here on earth. I wanted to show those connections" (Bennets, "Behind Lily Tomlin, Another Star").

Wagner's attempt, then, was to write a specific kind of comedy, one that makes a philosophical statement. She explained in another interview that she hoped to find a way of "balancing black humor and sentimentality." "We wanted a reflection, a balance of the absurdity and the realism," she said, "and we decided that after all, what is more absurd than real life?" (Fein). *The Search* sets up a dialectic between pessimistic "black humor" based on isolation and a "sentimental" optimism based on the premise of a nonhierarchical world community. Like the traditional comedy described by Northrop Frye, the play's significance "is ultimately social significance, the establishing of a desirable society." Within Frye's taxonomy of comedies, it most closely resembles the "symposium," "whose vision moves toward an integration of society in a form like that of the symposium itself, the dialectic festivity which . . . is the controlling force that holds society together" (286).

The Search also, of course, departs dramatically from Frye's description of comedy in the specific form its "dialectic festivity" takes. "What normally happens" Frye says, speaking of the entire Western tradition of comic drama, "is that a young man wants a young woman, that his desire is resisted by some opposition, usually paternal, and that near the end of the play some twist in the plot enables the hero to have his will. . . . At the end of the play the device in the plot that brings hero and heroine together causes a new society to crystallize around the hero" (163). The romantic strain that Frye says is most characteristic of the more optimistic forms of comedy, such as the symposium, is completely excluded from *The Search.* In fact, the character Judith Beasley dismisses romance quite overtly in the course of her public-access-TV recommendation of the vibrator, "a kind of Hamburger Helper for the boudoir. . . . 'But doesn't it kill romance?' you say. And I say, 'What doesn't?'" (33).

Instead, the play's resolution reflects the spiraling, open-ended qualities of much of women's comic writing. In the end, Kate, the quintessential snob, shares a moment with a bag lady and two prostitutes, finally "seeing" them across economic and social barriers as Trudi demanded in the opening moments of the play. This moment of contact is mirrored by Trudi's description of the extraterrestrials who find the audience at the violin concert "art," and again by the character Lily's audience at the Plymouth Theatre, and presumably by the real audience again at the Plymouth Theatre watching the real Lily. Beyond this suggestion of infinitely spiraling communal relationships, however, no resolution is offered to any of the subplots in the play.

Yet, simply on the basis of the number of jokes included, *The Search* is the purest instance of comedy examined so far. The most extended subplot—Lyn's journal of the seventies and eighties—also presents perhaps the clearest example of how both humor and romance function in the play in both traditional and nontraditional ways. Like *Top Girls, The Search* satirizes forms of feminism in telling Lyn's story. Lyn's consciousness-raising group concludes that "women don't want to fight. As Marge says, 'We'd rather sit around in a circle and process'" (140). Yet the group's notion that "this is about moving the WHOLE species forward, not just half of it," is one that the play's larger frame espouses. The criticisms of sixties feminism revolve not around philosophy but around fads and fashions, such as wearing camouflage fatigues: "I mean, honey, you couldn't BE more antiwar, but if it weren't for army surplus you'd have *nothing* to wear" (143), and growing underarm and leg hair: "How did you *manage* that much growth? I mean, the Women's Movement is still *young*" (146). Such jokes are more appealing for the nostalgia they evoke in an audience of baby boomers than for any comment they make about the feminist movement.

Later, again like *Top Girls,* Lyn's story provides fuel for satirizing the ambitious woman executive who practices "'power dressing,' a new fashion trend where you wear something around the neck that looks sort of like a scarf and sort of like a tie and sort of like a ruffle and doesn't threaten anyone, because you don't look good in it" (183). Yet again, Lyn is much more sympathetically portrayed than *Top Girls'* Marlene as she attempts to juggle marriage, a career, and hyperactive twins, sighing, "If I'd known this is what it would be like to have it all, I might have been willing to settle for less" (184).

Lyn also provides the sole romance among *The Search's* many subplots, when she meets and marries Bob, "the truest feminist . . . the only man I've ever known who knew where he was when Sylvia Plath died" (158). Bob aspires to be a "holistic capitalist," but ends up selling what Edie characterizes as "New Age chotchkes." The couple's attempt to combine the morally responsible attitudes of the sixties and seventies with the Yuppie ambitions of the eighties strains their marriage, and ultimately Lyn loses Bob (to his aikido instructor), along with her job (to an outsider who takes the promotion she has been promised), and even her friend Marge (whose loneliness drives her to suicide). Certainly Lyn and Bob represent a failed romance. Lyn's discovery that Bob is not "so damn Zen after all; you're passive aggressive" (186), mirrors her larger disappointment in being unable to be "politically conscious and upwardly mobile at the same time" (193).

Yet the concluding scenes of Lyn's story hold out some hope for the future. She tells Bob that when she took their sons to see Santa Claus, one asked for a nuclear freeze for Christmas, and the other "yanked Santa's beard off and said, 'What animal got killed for this?' I knew you'd be proud. I mean, for a kid that age to have the spirit to confront Santa Claus on what he thought was a MORAL issue. . . . Well . . . Maybe we did *some* things right, after all" (195). Feminism and the related New Age philosophy are gently ribbed, but are not dismissed in this story. Lyn seems naive in her expectations that she can "have it all," but the ideals she holds are never rejected. For her, hope lies not in the happy ending of romance, but in the possibility that the next generation will carry on these ideals more successfully than she has done. In the last scene, she holds a rummage sale to clear out her home prior to the divorce, but she retains her autographed copy of the first *Ms.* magazine, and the T-shirt Bob was wearing when they met, which says, "Whales Save Us." Thus, she retains her loyalty to both the political activism of feminism in the early seventies and to the larger, global perspective that has since become feminism's predominant strain. Lyn's story, like the entire play, is structured as a comedy, but as an open-ended, antiromantic comedy.

The play's humor, too, reflects a characteristically female point of view. Freud described tendentious, or aggressive, wit as a typically male behavior, an observation since borne out by social scientists. McGhee, summarizing what has been observed in numerous studies, describes both making and responding to jokes as sex-specific behaviors. Until about age six, both sexes initiate humor equally often, but after that age, boys take the lead. Girls seem to understand that telling jokes is an aggressive act and therefore inappropriate to girls, and also that the teller of jokes tends to dominate the social situation. Since it is true across gender lines that those with lower status tell fewer jokes and more self-deprecating (rather than aggressive) ones, it is not surprising to find that this is also true of girls and of women in our society. Girls and women are also more "field responsive" in responding to humor. While they can explain objectively what is supposed to be funny in a joke as well as males, they are much more likely to laugh if those around them are laughing, too.

While these findings can be used to reinforce the old stereotype that "women have no sense of humor," other interpretations are possible. For example, while Freud considered that all jokes function alike in offering a momentary liberation of feeling, he distinguished between tendentious wit, which liberates aggression, and self-deprecating humor, which evades suffering by a triumph of the superego. As Freud describes this process,

> the super-ego inherits the parental function; it often holds the ego in strict subordination, and still actually treats it as the parents (or the father) treated the child in his early years. We obtain a dynamic explanation of the humorous attitude, therefore, if we conclude that it consists in the subject's removing the accent from his own ego and transferring it on to his super-ego. To the super-ego, thus inflated, the ego can appear tiny and all its interests trivial, and with this fresh distribution of energy it may be an easy matter for it to suppress the potential reactions of the ego. (218-219)

It is interesting to note in this passage the parenthetical process whereby the primary parent in the child's early years becomes the father—certainly not the usual arrangement in our society, much less in prewar Vienna! Setting aside this Freudian slip, however, we are left with Freud's description of self-deprecating humor as quite positive ("peculiarly liberating and elevating"), contrasting with the assumption of later psychologists that all self-deprecation is bad. Freud, of course, does not go on to relate his description of the superego's function in self-deprecating humor to the nurturant role usually taken by women (220). The connection, however, seems obvious, suggesting that once again, women's psychology has been defined as different from men's and therefore inferior, when it may have much to recommend it. Further, at least one behavioral study shows that women tend to regard the "self-disparager," whether male or female, in a more favorable light than men do, judging such a person "appealing, witty, intelligent," and suggesting (to me, at least) that women may choose the role of self-disparager for themselves, rather than having it thrust upon them (Zillman and Stocking, 152).

Regina Gagnier suggests that the "field dependence" of women's response to humor might similarly be viewed in a reversed, positive light when she describes the observation of one of her students, that "men are perceived in behavioral science as field insensitive, contextually unaware, and environmentally oblivious" (137). Gagnier also suggests but does not develop the notion that women's field dependence might be related to "women's fluid boundaries" as described by Chodorow. Gagnier's focus is on the relation of status to humor, developed through a cross-class analysis of humor in Victorian women's autobiographies. She concludes, "Working women find humor in cross-class scenarios disrupting the social order, and upper-class women in disrupting the codes and regulations of their own class. This suggests that women's humor tends toward anarchy rather than the status quo, to prolonged disruption rather than, in Freudian theory, momentary release" (145). The latter observation reinforces what has already been observed about the tendency toward open-endedness in women's comic writing (Little). The description of humor that disrupts the social order as specifically female is, however, more perplexing. As Regina Barreca observes:

> It is not revolutionary to claim that comedy raises questions concerning authority. . . . Comedy has often been linked to man's [*sic*] ability to transcend his oppression by laughing at his chains, linked to his satiric facility which enables him to suggest changes for his society, and related to his natural cycles of regeneration and renewal.

> It is of paramount importance to note that these linkings
> are *well within* the boundaries of the established literary
> and social laws, for all their trafficking with subversion.
> (11)

Barreca maintains that no real change in the society results
from male comedy, only a reaffirmation of the status quo in
a new generation. Women writers, she says, "can acknowledge, by the very form of their expression, that accepted
authority is not authoritative. They write comedies that de-
flate the language of the symbolic order. . . . Comedy is a way
women writers can reflect the absurdity of the dominant
ideology while undermining the very basis for its discourse"
(19).

The anthropologist Mary Douglas describes the social function of joking as always "frivolous," yet "potentially subver-
sive. Since its form consists of a victorious tilting of uncontrol
against control, it is an image of the levelling of hierarchy, the
triumph of intimacy over formality, of unofficial values over
official ones" (366). Describing the function of all joking
without distinguishing the gender of the joker, she writes that
the joker "lightens for everyone the oppressiveness of social
reality, demonstrates its arbitrariness by making light of formality in general, and expresses the creative possibilities of
the situation" (372).

Specifically, Douglas believes that jokes, in devaluing the
social structure, value instead the informal community of
women and men. "Whereas 'structure' is differentiated and
channels authority through the system, in the context of
"community,' roles are ambiguous, lacking hierarchy,
disorganised. . . . Laughter and jokes, since they attack classi-
fication and hierarchy, are obviously apt symbols for expressing community in this sense of unhierarchised, undifferenti-
ated social relations" (370). Douglas describes joking as a kind
of "anti-rite" that reinforces this "unhierarchised" community, and the joker as a kind of minor mystic. In Douglas's view,
all jokers, "by revealing the arbitrary, provisional nature of the
very categories of thought, by lifting their pressure for a

moment and suggesting other ways of structuring reality"
present the possibility of an alternative society (374).

Women, because of their similar experiences, are likely to
hold some views in common as to what that alternative ought
to be. Women, because they have been silenced, have had less
opportunity to share their views. It is in these senses, I believe,
rather than through a high score on some scale of relative
subversiveness, that a "women's comedy" can be said to exist.
The Search is, in these senses, a clear example of such a
comedy. *The Well of Horniness,* while much less commercial
and more wildly farcical, offers another such example for
consideration.

The Well of Horniness by Holly Hughes, the very title of
which parodies Radclyffe Hall's somber lesbian classic, *The
Well of Loneliness,* also parodies the soap opera, the detective
thriller, pornographic films about lesbians, and radio and TV
commercials, in three brief "parts" amounting to twenty-six
pages in the published version. *The Well* was first performed
live at the WOW Café in New York City on March 3, 1983. It
has since been produced as a radio broadcast and as a live radio
play with actors performing all the sound effects on stage. All
the roles are performed by women, and the author notes, "I'm
pretty tough about this part. No men in *The Well,* okay?. . .
But there's a plus: academics just love this kind of stuff—
cross-dressing, women playing men. It's your entrée into
avant-garde circles, if you don't mind walking in circles"
(222).

As this introduction would suggest, the plot of *The Well* is
filled with patent absurdities. The story begins when Vicki, a
"reformed" lesbian and her fiancé, Rod, meet his sister,
Georgette, at a restaurant. Vicki fears that Georgette, also a
lesbian, will reveal her true identity. At the restaurant, Georgette
is first confronted by Babs, a rejected former lover who is now
a waitress. Georgette and Vicki then engage in a covert
seduction under the restaurant table. Georgette disappears
into the ladies' room. Vicki follows moments later, and discovers Georgette's dead body there. Vicki flees, fearing she will

be accused of the murder. In the woods outside town, she meets Georgette's lost twin, Dinette, who has been raised by raccoons, and the two women become lovers.

Detective Garnet McClit is assigned to investigate Georgette's murder. She meets Babs, who knocks her unconscious. Meanwhile, in the woods, Vicki is struck by a golf ball from a nearby tournament, and loses her memory. She is rushed to the hospital, where she is first knocked out by an injection from Babs (who uses her status as a temporary worker to turn up everywhere), and then is sexually attacked by female hospital workers "searching" her. Babs finds Rod and knocks him out, so that he misses Vicki's arraignment, and Vicki is convicted of Georgette's murder. The chief of police, a friend of Rod, tries to help Vicki for Rod's sake, but she elects prison, where she is sexually attacked by female prisoners. Garnet realizes that Babs must be the real murderer, and brings Vicki out of prison. The radio dispatcher interrupts Vicki and Garnet's love scene in Garnet's car to send them to Rod's carpet warehouse—but the dispatcher is Babs. In the carpet warehouse, a shot rings out, but it is not clear whether Rod or Vicki has been shot when Vicki is awakened by Rod. It has all been a bad dream. Rod and Vicki leave together for a restaurant.

The Well is loaded with double entendres and in-jokes of the lesbian subculture. Hughes clearly had no more serious intention than amusing her friends when she composed it, after "too many Bloody Marys," as she notes in the introduction. "There was to be no 'art' involved" (222). She has gone on to write more seriously intended plays for others and for her own one-woman performances. As she notes, "Now I'm older, no wiser, but infinitely more pretentious" (222). In June of 1990, Hughes became one of the "NEA Four" when she was rejected for a grant from the National Endowment for the Arts, after a recommendation from the endowment's theatre panel. While touring with a new, one-woman show called "World Without End," she told a newspaper interviewer, "People are saying, 'This is going to be the best thing that ever happened to your career.' But I can't help but think of other artists who came under attack—like Lenny Bruce, Oscar Wilde—and they spent the rest of their lives, which wasn't very long, trying to stay out of prison."

Jill Dolan finds in Hughes's work some of the purest examples of "materialist theatre." Dolan believes that simply representing the lesbian as subject can "denaturalize dominant codes by signifying an existence that belies the entire structure of the heterosexual culture and its representations" (116). Certainly *The Well* provides an example of the joke as "anti-rite" described by Douglas. The play's insistent parody of conventional romantic forms reveals their arbitrary and hierarchical nature. As Dolan points out, it is the casting of lesbians in traditionally male romantic roles that creates the challenge to heterosexual culture. Garnet McClit, "lady dick," provides the perfect heterosexual oxymoron.

Yet *The Well*'s structure is one that seems at first glance to resemble Frye's traditional comedy more than it does most women's comedy. The heterosexual couple, Rod and Vicki, are reunited in the final scene. All the lesbian characters and their disruptions of this "natural order" were, we are told, merely a dream, in a comic resolution that is positively Shakespearean in its contrivance. Only the couple's destination—a restaurant, just as in the opening scene—strikes an ominous note. Are they destined to reenact the events of the play on their arrival at the restaurant? Was Vicki's dream premonitory? Obviously, the conclusion, like every other element of the play, is parody, a playful exploitation of patriarchal conventions.

In the same way, romance in *The Well*—and it is rife with steamy scenes—is played for laughs. All the sex scenes either show lesbians behaving like heterosexual movie lovers (as Garnet and Vicki do in the car) or lesbians behaving as they do in pornographic movies intended for heterosexual male audiences (as in the prison and hospital scenes.) Even Rod and Vicki's reunion would be undercut in performance by Rod's portrayal by a woman.

A more seriously romantic portrayal of lesbian love is Jane

Chambers's *Last Summer at Bluefish Cove*. While *Last Summer*'s style is realistic (in marked contrast to *The Well*), the two plays bear striking similarities as well. Both plays use a whimsical, nonconfrontive style of humor, though *The Well* is broadly farcical while *Last Summer* is bittersweet. Neither the patriarchy nor men are directly attacked in either play. Instead, the humor derives from the absurdities the lesbian subjects reveal as individuals or from their absurd encounters with the patriarchal system. Both plays, like *The Search,* are thus examples of the deliberately self-deprecating style that has traditionally been characteristic of women. At the same time, they subtly undermine the patriarchal system through humor.

As Hughes observed in an interview, "Humor is a theatre tool. You can use it to dig deeper or to seduce the audience, to get them on your side—or as avoidance." While she attempts to use humor with "a why behind it," she rejects overt didacticism: "I really think politically correct drama is no drama." Chambers's attempt seems to have been to use romance as Hughes uses humor: as a form of seduction to her own point of view. Like Hughes, she borrows the conventions of heterosexual romance to tell a lesbian-centered story. But unlike *The Well, Last Summer* tells a charming but ultimately serious story of true love found and lost again.

Last Summer at Bluefish Cove was first produced by The Glines, opening February 13, 1980, at the Shandol Theatre, New York City. This production was revived June 3, 1980, at the West Side Mainstage, New York City, as part of the First American Gay Arts Festival. In December 1980, it was produced with a different cast by the Actors Playhouse in New York City, where it ran from December 22 through March 1, 1981.

Last Summer opens with Lil, fishing alone on Bluefish Cove. When Eva strolls down the beach, Lil strikes up a conversation. Interpreting Eva's manner as flirtatious, Lil invites her to a party at her cabin that night. In fact, Eva has fled to Bluefish Cove following the breakup of her marriage. She thinks of herself as heterosexual and is hoping—at least on a conscious level—only for a friendship with Lil.

A series of comic misunderstandings ensue at the party, followed by an explanation of the real situation: Bluefish Cove is the summer home of a community of lesbian women, several of them quite successful in different fields, most of them in long-term relationships. Only Lil is unattached at the moment, and struggling with feelings that she has done nothing worthwhile with her life. She and Eva fall in love and move in together. After a month of happiness, Lil falls sick and is forced to reveal to Eva what she and the rest of the community have been keeping secret: Lil is dying of cancer. The final scene of the play occurs in winter, shortly after Lil's funeral, when her friends come to clean out the cabin. Eva, the last to leave, assures the others, "I can make it by myself" (107).

Dolan argues that the play is in the tradition of gay coming-out stories, which focus on the protagonist's struggle with the heterosexual society and therefore stress the deviance of the protagonist's departure from that society. In fact, *Last Summer* occurs entirely within the physical and psychological framework of a lesbian community. Very little is said and nothing is seen of Eva's departure from heterosexual society. The other characters warn her that she may experience rejection from her family and friends and suffer a legal disadvantage in settling her divorce if she makes her lesbianism public, but none of these eventualities is dramatized. The focus, instead, is on Eva's developing relationship with Lil, which is depicted as a playful, sexy, and highly romantic one, and on her growing bond with the lesbian community. While Lil and a few of the other women are supposed to have led promiscuous lives in the past, the community at present seems quite settled, mostly in relationships that are depicted as loving and secure.

The characters are highly individualized, with quirks that draw on the conventions of TV situation comedies. Similarly, the love relationship between Lil and Eva overcomes misunderstandings and misplaced pride to develop into a strong and supportive one, capable of coping with Lil's cancer and prevailing, somewhat in the tradition of a TV movie-of-the-week. Dolan criticizes this use of realistic conventions in *Last Summer*, maintaining that the play "never breaks loose from the heterosexual contract that founds representation" (110). Must the serious use of realistic conventions place *Last Summer* beyond the pale of feminist drama, as Dolan suggests?

Last Summer can certainly be said to speak for silenced women, for the lesbians are represented as sympathetic, oppressed members of the patriarchal society. Community is a theme that resounds in the play. While Eva will make it "on her own," it seems clear by the final scene that she has become a part of a very close, supportive community as well. Unlike many of the plays examined here, *Last Summer* does not struggle with larger political questions. Instead, rather like *'Night, Mother*, it uses a tight focus to look closely at women usually neglected even in realistic drama.

Last Summer is unique among the plays examined here in that it presents a full-blown romance, one which uses many heterosexual conventions to present a romance between two women. As Dolan suggests may be true of other plays with lesbian subjects, *Last Summer* thus functions to "denaturalize dominant codes by signifying an existence that belies the entire structure of heterosexual culture and its representations" (116). The rhetorical effect of using lesbian subjects in such a context is to assert the normality and even familiarity of these women's lives.

While it might, for that reason, seem primarily directed at a heterosexual audience, it found a receptive audience among lesbians as well. One reviewer reported:

> The play is a joy for lesbians and a revelation for heterosexual women. What a relief to see lesbians portrayed as serious and silly, strong and weak, superficial and sensitive, grasping and generous. At certain points, the audience literally gasped with recognition. (*Womanews*, 1982)

In other words, the realistic style and individuated characters

were perceived as a rhetorical strength of the play, which I
would consider a feminist play, though certainly one on the
apolitical end of the spectrum.

Last Summer makes a fascinating comparison with the romance novels that have achieved such widespread popularity
with female audiences. Janice Radway, in her ground-breaking *Reading the Romance,* has delineated the plot of the "ideal
romance" as described by a group of female romance readers
she surveyed. Briefly, the ideal romance plot begins when the
heroine—a young, sexually innocent woman—is thrown into
a position of social isolation. She meets the hero, who is a
leader among men, but both promiscuous with and cynical
about women. The hero and heroine are at first antagonistic
with one another, but after a separation of some sort, the hero
behaves tenderly to the heroine, and she reinterprets his
ambiguous behavior. The hero declares his love; the heroine
responds, and her identity is restored, now as wife and future
mother (134).

Similarly, *Last Summer* begins with the arrival of Eva, who
by leaving her husband has destroyed her social identity.
Despite her married state, she is, like the heroine of a romance
novel, sexually innocent, while Lil describes her past life as
that of a promiscuous "alley cat" (25), much like the hero of
romance. Like him, too, she is presented sympathetically
despite this behavior, which is justified on the grounds that
neither she nor he has ever truly been in love before. Lil
behaves antagonistically toward Eva when they meet alone
after the disastrous party (50); later, the lovers are separated
by Lil's hospitalization.

Despite the similarities between these plots and characters,
important differences emerge as well. The heroine is clearly
the sole protagonist of romance novels, while the hero is the
inexplicable "other" to whom she reacts. *Last Summer,* in
contrast, is rather equally balanced between Eva and Lil, with
the audience privy at times to each one's private thoughts,
either as expressed to other characters or to each other.
Despite the heroine's primacy in conventional romance, she is

ultimately the passive partner who waits for the hero's declaration of love. Eva seems at first to play the role of the innocent heroine, but she is far from passive. It is Eva who kindles the romance by returning to Lil's room after the party, and the ultimate declaration of committed love comes from Eva as well. When Lil returns from the hospital, she tries again to make Eva leave, but Eva resists her, saying, "That's always worked for you, hasn't it? One act of bravado and you're off the hook" (102-103). Eva insists that she will stay with Lil to the end, and the scene ends with Eva holding Lil as she once held her little son, now dead. The stage directions observe that "Eva is now the strong one."

Finally, the romance novel ends "happily ever after" with a wedding, not with a funeral, as *Last Summer* does. If lovers in conventional romance are parted by death, it is assumed that their love will continue beyond the grave. Eva makes no such claim of eternal fidelity in the final scenes. On the other hand, Lil has felt that she will leave neither accomplishments nor children behind as her immortality. But Eva is seen to have been strengthened and enriched by her relationship with Lil, preparing her to go on with her life alone, yet supported by the women's community. Eva, then, is Lil's immortality, providing an appropriately bittersweet ending to their romance.

Radway relates the popularity of the romance novel's plot to the experience of female development as described by Chodorow. Because daughters tend to maintain preoedipal ties to their mothers throughout the oedipal period, they become erotically heterosexual but continue to need and desire their mothers emotionally into adulthood. Sons, in contrast, repress their oedipal ties with their mothers, define their personality by autonomy and independence, and often are constitutionally incapable of providing emotional nurturance. The basic asymmetry in male and female personality, Chodorow maintains, results in marriages that are emotionally unsatisfying to women, and explains a woman's desire and need to mother a child. Radway observes,

Although Chodorow emphasizes the effectiveness and success of mothering as an activity that compensates for the male inability to nurture, many women have also testified to the hidden costs of such a route to fulfillment. The activity of nurturing a child may indeed help to satisfy the female need for a self-in-relation and provide vicarious regression and affection, but it also makes tremendous demands on a woman to focus on the infant rather than on herself. . . . Given the nature of the female personality as a self-in-relation, the inability of men to function as completely adequate relational partners, and reciprocal demands made upon women by the very children they rely on to satisfy their unmet needs, it is understandable that many women derive pleasure and encouragement from repetitive indulgence in romantic fantasies. On one level, then, the romance is an account of a woman's journey to female personhood *as that particular psychic configuration is constructed and realized within patriarchal culture.* (137-138)

In this context, *Last Summer* emerges as an alternate route to "female personhood" for Eva, via her relationship with Lil. Eva's marriage has apparently failed for the reasons Chodorow describes. Continuing her quest for an "adequate relational partner" with whom she can reenact the emotional intimacy of her preoedipal relationship with her mother, Eva finds both emotional and sexual satisfaction with a woman. Lil, despite a seemingly different background, follows a similar progression. Having presumably grown up in an intimate relationship with her mother, she describes herself in adulthood as having been unable to make an intimate connection. For her, Eva is both a child she can teach about lovemaking and a mother to whom she can admit her emotional needs. If Radway is correct in finding a quest for the preoedipal mother behind conventional romance, then *Last Summer,* in which two women find each other, is the women's romance both deconventionalized and brought to psychological perfection.

From *The Search*'s cheerful dismissal of romance to *The Well*'s wicked parody to *Last Summer*'s lesbian revision, feminist dramatists in the eighties can be seen tackling the subject of romance from every direction, rejecting, adapting or poking fun at the plot structure traditionally supposed to be the special realm to which women authors and audiences would be confined. At the same time, these authors have invaded the supposedly male realm of humor, bringing to bear the wise woman's sense of self-deprecation, along with the outsider's ability to question the absurdities of the patriarchy. All three of these plays employ the structures and strategies of contemporary feminist drama, and in a remarkable achievement, add to them a distinctly feminist comic twist.

8 • Summary and Conclusions

> In the future, art will continue to reflect the progress of
> social movements in its rhetorical motives, as Burke has
> observed. If feminism continues to evolve, aspects of its
> ideology now familiar to only a few may become appar-
> ent to the larger society. When that happens, playwrights
> observant of society may create a drama without either
> the ideological or the artistic limitations of the drama
> examined here. A new form of feminist drama will then
> fully emerge that will artfully express the possibility of
> woman's autonomy. (Brown, 145)

In 1979 I concluded *Feminist Drama* with these words. Feminism has indeed continued to evolve since then into a complex
philosophy with political, psychological, and moral implications for the whole human race and for the life of our planet
itself.

Historians have begun to recover the lost voices of women
of the past, while they have redefined the meaning of history
itself by focusing on the daily lives of common people.
Psychologists have revealed that women's psychological and
ethical development is not simply a defective version of men's,
but instead follows its own distinctive pattern of development.
The insights of Freud, of Marx, and of Jesus have been both
criticized and analyzed for their usefulness in understanding
woman's place in society. Political theorists offer strategies for
making the changes in society that ethicists believe women
have envisioned first and have held most deeply.

Many aspects of feminist ideology are accepted now by the
larger society, as evidenced by the appearance of the plays

examined here on and off Broadway and in regional theatres across the country. The final hurdle to mass popularity—commercial film—is now being cleared by these and similar properties. 'Night, Mother, for instance, whose middle-aged female characters and somber theme would have been unthinkable even on stage a decade ago, has been made into a film starring Sissy Spacek and Geraldine Fitzgerald. One of the newest of the plays considered here—The Stick Wife—is, according to Cloud's agent, already being sought as a film property. Yet The Stick Wife, like the other plays examined here, resolutely avoids the easy commercial appeal of a glamorous protagonist involved in an action-oriented plot.

Instead, the play is a dissection of the nexus between racism and sexism, revealed in the moral dilemma of a Klansman's wife. Jessie draws strength to face the truth of her husband's behavior from the community of housewives in her working-class neighborhood. Although these women throw their aprons over their heads and refuse to answer each others' phone calls in farcical efforts to evade this knowledge, they also seek each other out with the awful news, apparently feeling that only by being shared can it be borne. Their shared sense of unarticulated connection with the grieving black mothers exemplifies traditional female psychology. But while the other women are seemingly frozen into postures of submissive grief, Jessie finds the strength to act—to bear witness against her husband's crime, thus risking her own livelihood and perhaps her life. She does not resist but rather transcends the meaningless boredom of housework in pursuit of her moral and spiritual self.

Clearly, Jessie is not motivated by abstract principle—the only principles expressed in the play are those held by the Klansmen. Jessie seems no more capable of debating these than she is of living her life by them. Rather she is motivated by her sense of relationship, by an ethic of care that expands, following her decision, from care for others to an interrelated caring for herself. Although she is living on the margins both of society and of sanity, Jessie is imbued by a sense of her own right to survival and even to self-expression that seemingly will carry over into her marriage at the play's end. Thus she exemplifies contemporary feminism's ethical sense that self and other, indeed all living things, are related.

Despite the deep seriousness of the subject, *The Stick Wife* is imbued with a slapstick style of humor reminiscent of *I Love Lucy*. Like Lucy Ricardo and Ethel Mertz, hoping to meet movie stars and make a million dollars selling salad dressing, the women in this play are presented as fools, with their dreams of kissing Gary Cooper and their ignorance of the patriarchy. But unlike Lucy and Ethel, who return at the end of each episode to condescending but harmless husbands, Jessie and her friends return at the end of the play to live with members of the Ku Klux Klan. The dangers and difficulties of acquiring forbidden knowledge are, for these women, both real and imminent. Moreover, Jessie and, to a lesser extent, her friends, do overcome the considerable barriers presented, to learn and to speak about the evils that surround them.

Thus, though these characters are built on the denigrating image of the dumb housewife, the real target of the satire is not the women, but the society that insists on keeping them helplessly ignorant. The trivial slights to the wives—the stuff of situation comedy—are seen to derive from the same impulse that bombs churches and kills black children.

When Jessie goes mad, the norms of the patriarchal society are thrown further into question. What seems at first to be a crazy insistence on living in the backyard turns out to be simple self-protectiveness: a house, unlike a yard, can be bombed. In the "women's camp" she and her friends create, the values of the patriarchy are overturned. The women speak the truth to each other, creating the exhilarating humor of the "anti-rite" described by Douglas, in which a nonhierarchical community questions the values of the hierarchy and, for a moment, calls the whole society into question.

The transformative powers and stifling constrictions of community form the themes of *For Colored Girls* and *The Brothers*. Revolving in each case around a group of black women, the two plays mirror each other in reverse images. While *For Colored Girls* celebrates speech, *The Brothers* mourns silence. *For Colored Girls* finds hope in black sisterhood for the ultimate transformation of society, while *The Brothers* portrays the hopelessness of black competition in the white patriarchal society. The women in *The Brothers* seem bound to history: just as the play itself is framed by the deaths of Gandhi and King, so the characters are hemmed in by the particulars of their historical moment. *For Colored Girls,* in contrast, seems to evolve almost spontaneously, in real time, and concludes by looking resolutely toward the future.

Each play makes its own use of humor. In *For Colored Girls,* the women make fun of their own willingness to put up with the inadequacies of their lovers. Their innocence in the face of the impositions of the patriarchy is revealed to them in the course of the play, and sharing the joke seems to give them the courage to put this behavior behind them. Thus, the humor that at first seems to denigrate the women themselves eventually is seen to be symptomatic of the larger society. The women in *The Brothers* make frequent jokes— mostly of what Freud would call the "tendentious" type. The central "joke" is, of course, that Nelson is trying to smother himself with his pillow, a notion finally acted out with deadly seriousness by his wife at the end of the play. In *For Colored Girls,* the women use humor to transform themselves. In *The Brothers,* the women use humor to help them bear their situation; no one moves on.

The plays share a great deal as well: an emphasis on the emergence into speech of silenced black women; a warning against class barriers within what should be a unified black community; and a painfully honest analysis of the relationship between racism and sexism, this time from the black woman's point of view. While both plays pointedly avoid portrayal of white characters or their viewpoints, the plays nevertheless make a strong argument for the value of connection, at least among minority women. The strength to rise above their oppressive circumstances and make those connections will come, these plays suggest, from black women with a sense of their own self-worth and of the strength of their community.

The Brothers and *For Colored Girls* exemplify the "communal play," a distinctively feminist form in which a group shares the role of protagonist. In this form, the audience receives a panoramic view of many women's lives. In contrast, *Getting Out* and especially *'Night, Mother* take an almost microscopically detailed look at the lives of individual women facing their most personal crises. While the characters in Norman's plays are by no means politicized heroines struggling to transform society, their struggles simply to survive with integrity intact make a telling comment on society's need for change.

Further, the protagonists' circumstances in both plays are so extreme that their struggles do finally assume heroic proportions. For Arlene, resisting the pressure to return to prostitution and thus remove herself from the dirty apartment and dead-end jobs that are all the "straight" life has to offer begins as an effort to reclaim custody of her son, thus to reclaim her own role as mother. The scene between Arlene and her mother illustrates the severely limited nurturance that Arlene herself received. Not until she accepts the nurture of her neighbor, Ruby, can Arlene forgive and accept her own child self. By learning to accept herself, she takes the first step toward mothering her child. Thus, as Gilligan observes, the line between caring for others and caring for self is dissolved.

This dissolution is most movingly illustrated in the final moments of *Getting Out,* when the adult Arlene is reunited with her child self—by means of humor. Arlie's story of being locked in the closet, and taking her revenge by peeing in her mother's shoes, strikes Arlene as funny, and the "two" share a laugh. By laughing at her younger self, Arlene accepts and forgives herself, in a perfect example of the type of humor Freud describes as "liberating"—the humor of self-deprecation. The superego, here represented by the conscientious Arlene, adopts a parental attitude toward the ego, represented by Arlie. Freud notes that in other respects the superego is "a stern master. . . . If it is really the super-ego which, in humor, speaks such kindly words of comfort to the intimidated ego, this teaches us that we have still very much to learn about the nature of that agency" (220-221). In particular, Freud had yet to learn the peculiar appropriateness of this form of humor to female psychology. In this moment, Arlene "mothers" herself—just as feminists since the sixties have been urging women to do. The emotionally orphaned Arlene, it seems, will win the right to mother her son by first learning to mother herself.

'*Night, Mother,* too, revolves around a mother/child relationship, this time a more literal one. Although Jessie is now an adult, on the night of her suicide she has reduced the world of others to the infant's: she will answer for her decision only to her mother. Jessie's struggle in the play is to separate herself from her mother while at the same time she offers her compassionate support. Jessie understands that only by comprehending their separation will her mother be freed from guilt and responsibility for Jessie's death. Mama grows in the course of the play into an acceptance of Jessie's power to dispose of her own life as she chooses.

Before she reaches this final acceptance, however, Mama, too, seizes on humor in her effort to rescue her child. Describing her best friend, Agnes, to Jessie, she insists that Agnes keeps a houseful of birds, wears whistles around her neck, eats okra twice daily, and has burned down her last eight homes. When Jessie refuses to believe that Agnes would put up porch chairs and make lemonade for the spectators at these fires, Mama responds, "Be exciting, though, if she did. You never know" (40). Later, she defends her lies by saying: "I only told you about it because I thought I might get a laugh out of you for once even if wasn't the truth, Jessie. Things don't have to be true to talk about 'em, you know" (41). Mama is, in fact, demonstrating to Jessie two more reasons to live: for the fun of making up tall stories, and for the delight of life's unexpectedness, because "you never know."

Nearly all the plays considered in this volume focus on women whom circumstances of race, class, or character have seemingly rendered powerless. Yet in Norman's plays, as in *The Stick Wife* and in *For Colored Girls,* these women find a way to exercise control over their own lives and influence on those around them. *In The Boom Boom Room* provides an interesting contrast in this regard. In *Boom Boom Room,* Chrissy struggles toward a dimly conceived autonomy against an upbringing and an environment that have insistently objectified and degraded her. By the climax of the play, she has reached her first conscious anger at this treatment—an anger for which she is violently reprimanded and effectively silenced.

In *Hurlyburly,* written ten years later, most of the women have no more power, wealth, or education than Chrissy has. Certainly they are held in no greater regard by the men in the play than Chrissy is by the denizens of the Boom Boom Room. Both Chrissy and Donna seem initially to be stereotypical "dumb blondes" or "bimbos," and humor in the early scenes of both plays derives from their apparent vacuousness. In fact, both turn out to be far wiser than the more powerful people who surround them. Donna, in particular, is an almost perfect example of the "wise fool" in female form.

The wise fool who is female has been a consistent character in our popular culture (i.e., the character played by Gracie Allen), yet I have found no critical recognition of the existence of such a character. William Willeford, in his classic work on the fool, describes him as possessing feminine characteristics, engaging in cross-dressing, even as hermaphroditic, but never suggests that the fool might be played by a female.

Fools, according to Willeford, burlesque the sacred, including authority, sexuality, misfortune, and foreigners (or outsiders to the society). The fool is assigned the status of object in the subject/object split, and thus is associated with the unconscious, the feminine, and nature. The fool has infantile qualities because he draws on childhood, a past to which most of us have closed ourselves on the conscious level. Yet the fool can speak wisdom. Willeford describes a fool-hero who commits himself "to the irrational flow of life," and who inspires identification and even admiration in the audience.

Donna—the child-woman, the sex object, the outsider—
has clear affinities with this character. In the final scene of
Hurlyburly, the philosophy she recommends to Eddie is, in
almost the same words Willeford uses, a commitment to life's
"irrational flow." It is not only Donna, however, who gradually wins the respect of the audience. All the women in *Hurlyburly*
seem to maintain a quiet sense of self-determination despite
the vulnerability of their circumstances. When Bonnie is
pushed out of her own car by Phil, she returns on foot to
reprimand Eddie for arranging their date. Phil's beleagured
wife, Susie, is able to override Phil's reluctance to have a baby.
Even Donna, a homeless teenager, walks out on her only
shelter when she is mistreated by Phil.

Yet the women in *Hurlyburly* are patient with the men, and
when they eventually assert themselves, it is without the
extreme aggression that Chrissy shows in her final outburst.
Susie simply hangs up on Eddie after he has encouraged Phil's
hostile behavior. When Eddie becomes too possessive, Darlene
politely and regretfully breaks off their relationship. Nor do
the women seem to hold a grudge. Bonnie ends her tirade
against men by conceding that Artie may accompany her and
her daughter to Disneyland the next day. Donna drifts back
into the men's apartment a year after walking out on them with
the words, "Hey, Eddie! I ain't mad anymore. You mad?"
(161).

While the external circumstances in women's lives have not
changed in the ten years that separate the plays, their sense of
themselves apparently has. The philosophy Donna articulates
in the final scene of *Hurlyburly*—that "everything relates to
everything else, one way or another"—suggests by its lack of
ego and its fatalism that it has evolved from the very powerlessness of women's circumstances (162). In *Women and Spirituality,* Carol Ochs suggests,

> Women in most societies have long been relegated to
> conditions of powerlessness, servitude, and even suffer-
> ing. To insist that women must derive meaning from

their experiences as women in no way justifies or con-
dones these conditions. But people are always more than
what others have done to them. By exercising their
freedom and creativity, women can learn even from their
alienation, servitude, and degraded positions without in
any way accepting them or excusing those who brought
them about. (27)

This is evidently what Donna and perhaps all the women in
Hurlyburly have done. Donna's successful communication of
this philosophy to Eddie, a powerful, successful white male,
offers a glimmer of hope for the eventual transformation of
patriarchal society. In the final scene of *Hurlyburly,* the blind
patriarch receives a vision from the wise, female fool.

In *Top Girls,* Churchill presents us with two female fools,
one historical and one contemporary. In the opening dinner
party scene, Dull Gret is the outsider, the simpleton in a glib
and glittering company. Yet it is she who seems to have clung
to human values, while the women of greater status and
intelligence have lost their moral connections. Similarly, in
contemporary life, Marlene has lost her connection to her
sister and her daughter, as well as her sense of responsibility to
them and people like them. Angie, the fool, forecasts a
"frightening" future controlled by people like Marlene. But
Top Girls, unlike *Hurlyburly,* offers not even a moment of true
communication between Marlene and Angie, between the
powerful, conscious side and the powerless unconscious, the
unacknowledged daughter, the fool.

The Search for Signs of Intelligent Life in the Universe presents
yet another female fool in Trudi, the bag lady. The presenter
and, in a sense, the originator of all the other characters, she
suggests the character Willeford calls "the Mother of Fools," a
character who refuses to divide, define, or limit herself, and
"in whose worship every order of being is at one" (xvii). Like
the Mother of Fools, Trudi has an unbounded consciousness;
she sees into the minds of all the other characters, and even
communicates with aliens. All the other characters are "at

one" in their foolishness, of course, since this is plainly comedy, and comedy in which all the characters are fair game. They are "at one," as well, in the sense that they all inhabit Trudi's mind, and they are united at the deepest level by their common humanity. Again, the community of characters forms the protagonist of the play.

This community as protagonist, which Mary Douglas describes as the underlying assumption of comic behavior in society, is a persistent device in the plays examined here. Both *The Well of Horniness* and *Last Summer at Bluefish Cove* share this device, as well as the spiraling structure that is typical both of comedy in general and of women's writing in particular. Their parodies of romance plotting are in the comic tradition as well. Feminist playwrights are much more at home, it would seem, among the devices and structures of comedy than with those of tragedy.

Sue-Ellen Case seems to make a similar point when she suggests that women authors are singularly unsuited to the production of tragedy. She goes on, however, to argue that this is because

> tragedy [is] a replication of the male sexual experience. Tragedy is composed of foreplay, excitation and ejaculation (catharsis). The broader organisation of plot—complication, crisis and resolution—is also tied to this phallic experience. . . . A female form might embody her sexual mode, aligned with multiple orgasms, with no dramatic focus on ejaculation or necessity to build to a single climax. (129)

Case herself goes on at once to note the "essentialist" nature of this idea, based on female biology and seeming to valorize a single "feminine" form.

A further objection could certainly be made: male playwrights today are not writing tragedy, either. In fact, it might be observed (most obviously in Rabe, but other examples abound), that the characteristics I have identified as true of women writers are true, in many instances, of contemporary

male playwrights as well. Certainly, the emphasis placed in
The Search on the follies of egotism and the values of connection and community are echoed less cheerfully but no less
tellingly in *Hurlyburly*, written by a man. This apparent para-
dox calls to mind the often-told anecdote about Ibsen's
response to the Norwegian Society for Women's Rights, who
chose to honor him for his authorship of *A Doll's House*. Ibsen
is usually represented as having simply denied any interest or
affiliation with the feminist movement. In fact, his response
was this:

> I must disclaim the honor of having consciously worked
> for women's rights. I am not even quite sure what
> women's rights really are. To me it has been a question of
> human rights. . . . Of course it is incidentally desirable to
> solve the problem of women; but that has not been my
> whole object. My task has been the portrayal of human
> beings. (Meyer, 64)

While a feminist ethic has developed as an expression of
women's psychology and experience, this expression has not
been limited to audiences of women. Rather, as women's work
has begun to enter the mainstream of commercial theatre, the
feminist ethic has become a strain in the larger culture,
available to both male and female authors.

One might draw a somewhat inexact analogy to the cultural
process by which the arts of a foreign culture are introduced
into a new land by the natives of that culture. For a period of
time, only these native immigrants perform in "their" style.
But soon these performances attract admirers and imitators,
while the immigrants begin to alter their performances to
include what they are now seeing and hearing. In the same
way, I believe that a female perspective is entering the mainstream of American culture, where it is, of course, surrounded
by other, sometimes contradictory views. Nevertheless, it is
now available to authors and to audiences in unprecedented
numbers. Thus, men's use of structures, subjects, and points

of view identified as female in origin, far from disproving the existence of a distinctly female viewpoint, demonstrates the growth of this female viewpoint into a feminist viewpoint, detectible in the work of both women and men.

While Case is reluctant to rule out tragedy as a form available to feminists, she feels no such reluctance in eliminating the genre of realism. "Realism," she writes, "in its focus on the domestic sphere and the family unit, reifies the male as sexual subject and the female as the sexual 'Other.'" Jeanie Forte, in an article entitled "Realism, Narrative, and the Feminist Playwright," declares that realism, "always a reinscription of the dominant order, could not be useful for feminists" (116).

Of the plays examined here, *The Brothers, 'Night, Mother, Boom Boom Room* (except for its short, fragmented scenes), *Hurlyburly,* and *Bluefish Cove* fall squarely into the category of realism. *For Colored Girls, The Search for Signs,* and *The Well of Horniness* are clearly nonrealistic. The remainder use realistic dialogue and settings, but also include some nonrealistic devices: the split protagonist in *Getting Out,* the historical dinner party that opens *Top Girls,* the ghosts of light in *Stick Wife.* Yet all these plays, I believe, are examples of feminist drama. Some are more politically oriented than others, but the more political plays are not necessarily the less realistic ones. It is when the realistic plays are regarded in the light of Forte's definition of realism that the reason for this disjuncture becomes clear.

Forte defines realism, not according to any theorist or practitioner of the genre, but according to Catherine Belsey, writing in *Feminist Criticism and Social Change.* Realistic drama, according to Belsey and Forte, is characterized by "illusionism," and by a plot in which disorder is precipitated in the "signifying systems," followed by the reestablishment of order at the end of the drama. The dominant ideology is invariably supported by such a drama, for two reasons. First, the reader is constructed as an individual subject—presumed to be male—within the ideology. Second, the realistic drama poses an apparently objective viewpoint from which narrator and reader assess meaning. This "pose makes the operations of ideology covert, since the illusion is created for the reader that he or she is the source of meaning or understanding, unfettered by structures of culture" (115).

The plays I have identified as realistic are certainly guilty of illusionism—that is, of presenting their events as a truthful representation of the real world, in which the author remains an impersonal observer. This was the goal of the first realists in the nineteenth century, and it remains the hallmark of realism. Those early realists would have denied that this viewpoint was a "pose" to hide the operations of ideology; nevertheless, they were accused from the first of covertly didactic intentions—that is, of presenting a critique of societal problems, including the capitalist system, the double standard of sexual behavior, and the legal rights of women. Certainly, much realistic drama today supports the dominant ideology. But nowhere does Forte explain why a feminist ideology might not adopt realism's pose of objectivity in support of its own ends. Indeed, Patricia Schroeder suggests that a "modified" realism might be uniquely suited to some forms of feminist drama, noting that "the proscenium stage offers playwrights built-in opportunities for dramatizing the traditional systems of enclosure that restrict women" (111-112).

Nor does Forte explain why the subject to whom realistic drama is directed must be male—although that has most often been the case. Forte herself remarks that male and female readers have had quite disparate reactions to 'Night, Mother, certainly a pure instance of realism. Women have been generally more sympathetic, she notes, without considering the possibility that this is because a woman is the intended subject of the drama. 'Night, Mother, like all of these plays, has modified and adapted traditional structures to address its own ends and its own audience.

The plot described by Forte as characteristic of realism, in which the dominant order is disrupted by the "motivating force of Oedipal desire" and then is reinscribed, bears no more resemblance to the realistic plays examined here than to those which are nonrealistic. Nor is it particularly a characteristic of realism, although it does characterize much of Western drama, as both Burke and Frye have observed. Indeed, it is surprising that Forte could refer so often to Oedipus and yet avoid the contradiction to her argument that Sophocles' play presents. The plot of *Oedipus Rex* fits Forte's definition perfectly, but plainly, *Oedipus Rex* is a nonrealistic drama.

The plays examined here borrow from realism as from other conventions of Western drama, modifying and adapting them to their own rhetorical purposes. Building on the traditions of patriarchal Western drama, they bring to these traditions new values and fresh structural approaches. Most serious drama grapples with spiritual and ethical concerns. But these plays surprise and delight by their discovery of the spiritual in c-r groups and in housework, by their interpretation of the ethical not as a matter of principle but of care and by the humor with which they treat what has been regarded as serious and the seriousness with which they treat what has been regarded as trivial.

The revelation of the formerly secret lives of "bleeding stage managers," as *The Brothers'* Danielle calls women, gives these plays the spark of originality. Again and again, the "trivial" lives of housewives, go-go girls, and ex-convicts move into the foreground of these plays, while their husbands, boyfriends, and employers form the oppressive environment within which these unorthodox protagonists struggle to define themselves. Furthermore, this struggle is seldom the simple assertion of an autonomous ego found in much of patriarchal Western drama. Rather, these women assert themselves— often by "speaking up" when they had been silenced—both on others' behalf and as a consequence of others' support. The lady in red speaks in *For Colored Girls* on behalf of "the ghost of another woman / who waz missin what i waz missin" (50). Chrissy is finally moved to defiant speech in *Boom Boom Room* by her husband's verbal attack on a female telephone operator. And in *The Stick Wife,* Jessie "witnesses"—in both the

legal and the spiritual senses of that word—on behalf of four
bereaved black mothers whom she has never met.

For these characters, spiritual strength lies in community.
In *Getting Out,* Arlene finds real freedom when she finds a
female confidante in Ruby. In *The Stick Wife,* Jessie draws the
strength to defy the Klan from her coffee-klatch friends.
Women of color celebrate the strength of community in
spiritual terms in *For Colored Girls* and mourn its loss as a loss
of life itself in *The Brothers.* Chrissy in *Boom Boom Room*
struggles unsuccessfully for autonomy in isolation. In *Top
Girls,* Marlene demonstrates the moral wasteland that the
achievement of such isolated autonomy brings. Jessie in *'Night,
Mother* draws more than despair from her decision to die by
achieving what psychologists believe is a more characteristic
female goal—autonomy in connection.

Such a strong sense of connectedness must affect structure
as well, and often does in these plays, resulting in two protagonists, two actors portraying one protagonist, or a communal
protagonist made up of all the characters in the play. Even in
those plays with one clearly defined protagonist, the relative
importance of all the roles is more evenly distributed than in
most patriarchal Western drama. While the plot structure of
these plays, as of much women's writing, is spiraling, the plays
are by no means self-contained, circular exercises in absurdism. Rather, they present worlds that are resonant with meaning. Their characters struggle with moral responsibility for the
whole of society, or are condemned, as in *Top Girls* and *The
Brothers,* for their failure to do so.

Yet this drama never takes itself too seriously. Indeed,
nearly every play combines an unflinching portrayal of life's
darkest moments with a deadpan rendition of its most ridicu-
lous. Chrissy's longing in *Boom Boom Room* to find artistic
fulfillment through go-go dancing combines the poignance
and the absurdity of a classic fool. In *For Colored Girls,* the lady
in orange caps off a bitter recrimination of her lover with a
flippant observation: "i cdnt stand bein sorry & colored at the
same time / it's so redundant in the modern world." And in

'Night, Mother Jessie can interrupt discussion of her own planned suicide to tease her mother gently. Mama, still coming to terms with Jessie's revelation, worries, "You didn't eat a bite of supper," and Jessie responds, "Does this mean I can't have any hot chocolate?"

Interestingly, while women are usually the central characters in these plays, the connections these women seek are not only with others like themselves. Rather, the plays reflect contemporary feminism's quest to cross lines of gender, race, class, and age—indeed, to include everyone, to conceive of the world itself as community. In *The Stick Wife,* a white, lower-class housewife sacrifices her husband and risks her life out of moral outrage at his murder of four black children. Yet the playwright is careful to include the sense of social exclusion and worthlessness that motivated the husband as well. In *Top Girls,* the real heroines are not the "high-visibility" executives and adventurers, but the working-class women who struggle on behalf of their families and neighbors. It is emblematic of this new inclusiveness that David Rabe's work bears so much similarity to these plays by women. In *Hurlyburly,* Eddie begins to unravel the moral chaos of Hollywood by attending to the words of a teenage girl he had previously dismissed as a simpleminded sex object. Those words, significantly, are that "everything pertains to everything else one way or another."

Thus, as all these plays do, *Hurlyburly* expresses an "ethic of care" derived in part, at least, from the domestic experiences of women—experiences that society has often trivialized, but in which women have nevertheless found moral and even spiritual significance. The world of housework can be a sacred refuge, as in *The Stick Wife;* a meaningful alternative to the alienated world of paid work, as in *Top Girls;* or a resonant metaphor for life itself, as in *'Night, Mother.* Children, traditionally a peripheral concern of patriarchal Western drama, are central to many of these plays. The crisis in *For Colored Girls* comes when Crystal watches Beau Willie hold their children out the open window. Just as the death of a child in

The Brothers symbolizes the death of her parents' marriage, the existence of a child in *Getting Out* gives Arlene a reason to live and "go straight." The adolescents in *Hurlyburly* and *Top Girls,* although powerless and exploited, understand the value of connection and so represent our best hope for the future, however faint that hope may be.

By their commercial and critical success, these plays suggest that hope for the future need not be so faint as feminists have sometimes feared. The expansion of feminism into a global vision and the proliferation of that vision in popular drama are clearly visible over as short a time span as the last ten years. Yet these plays warn that women, merely by being women, hold no automatic moral advantage, nor will a narrowly conceived, selfishly motivated feminism effect any transformation of society. Only through the moral courage to witness on behalf of the whole of humanity as these plays do, and to hear that witness as audiences are now beginning to do, will this vision ever be realized.

Works Cited

Abel, Elizabeth; Marianne Hirsch; and Elizabeth Langland, eds. *The Voyage In: Fictions of Female Development*. Hanover, NH: University Press of New England, 1983.

Barreca, Regina, ed. *Last Laughs: Perspectives on Women and Comedy*. Studies in Gender and Culture 2. New York: Gordon and Breach, 1988.

Belsey, Catherine. "Constructing the Subject; Deconstructing the Text." In *Feminist Criticism and Social Change: Sex, Class and Race in Literature and Culture,* eds. Judith L. Newton and Deborah S. Rosenfelt. London, 1985.

Bennets, Leslie. "Behind Lily Tomlin, Another Star." *New York Times,* 4 Oct. 1985: 3: 4.

———. "The 7 'Top Girls' Speak Out." *New York Times,* 6 Jan. 1983: C15.

Brockett, Oscar. *History of the Theatre*. 4th ed. New York: Allyn and Bacon, 1982.

Brown, Janet. *Feminist Drama: Definition and Critical Analysis*. Metuchen, NJ: Scarecrow Press, 1979.

Brownstein, Rachel M. "Jane Austen: Irony and Authority." In *Last Laughs: Perspectives on Women and Comedy*, ed. Regina Barreca. New York: Gordon and Breach, 1988. 57-70.

Burke, Kenneth. *The Philosophy of Literary Form.* New York: Vintage Books, 1957-1961.

Caldwell, Susan Havens. "Experiencing the Dinner Party." *Women's Art Journal* 1-2 (1980-1981): 35-37.

Case, Sue-Ellen. *Feminism and Theatre.* New York: Methuen, 1988.

Chambers, Jane. *Last Summer at Bluefish Cove.* The JH Press Gay Play Script Series. New York: JH Press, 1982.

Chicago, Judy. *The Dinner Party: A Symbol of our Heritage.* Garden City, NY: Anchor Press, 1979.

Chinoy, Helen Krich, and Linda Walsh Jenkins. *Women in American Theatre.* 2nd ed. New York: Theatre Communications Group, 1987.

Chodorow, Nancy. *The Reproduction of Mothering: Psychoanalysis and the Sociology of Gender.* Berkeley: University of California Press, 1978.

Christ, Carol P. *Diving Deep and Surfacing: Women Writers on Spiritual Quest.* Boston: Beacon Press, 1980.

Christian, Barbara. *Black Feminist Criticism: Perspectives on Black Women Writers.* New York: Pergamon Press, 1985.

Churchill, Caryl. *Top Girls.* London: Methuen, 1982.

Cloud, Darrah. *The Stick Wife.* Ms.

———. "The Stick Wife: From the Playwright." Hartford Stage Company program for *The Stick Wife.* 5.

———. "The Tough Life of a Klansman's Wife." Interview

with Janice Arkatov. *Los Angeles Times,* 14 Jan. 1987: Calendar 1.

Collins, Kathleen. *The Brothers.* In *Nine Plays by Black Women,* ed. Margaret B. Wilkerson. New York: New American Library, 1986.

Curb, Rosemary K. "Re/cognition, Re/presentation, Re/creation in Woman-Conscious Drama: The Seer, the Seen, the Scene, the Obscene." *Theatre Journal,* Oct. 1985. 303-316.

Dolan, Jill. *The Feminist Spectator as Critic.* Theatre and Dramatic Studies 52. Ann Arbor, MI: UMI Research Press, 1988.

Donovan, Josephine. *Feminist Theory: The Intellectual Traditions of American Feminism.* New York: Frederick Ungar, 1985.

Douglas, Mary. "The Social Control of Cognition: Some Factors in Joke Recognition." *Man* 3 (1968): 361-376.

DuPlessis, Rachel Blau. *Writing Beyond the Ending: Narrative Strategies of Twentieth-Century Writers.* Bloomington: Indiana University Press, 1985.

Eder, Richard. "Louisville Festival Offers 6 New Plays." Review of *Getting Out,* by Marsha Norman, and other plays. Actors Theatre Festival of New Plays. *New York Times,* 16 Nov. 1977, 3:21.

Ehrenreich, Barbara. "The Next Wave." *Ms.,* Aug. 1987: 166+.

Elshtain, Jean Bethke. *Public Man, Private Women: Women in*

Social and Political Thought. Princeton, NJ: Princeton University Press, 1981.

Fein, Esther B. "Lily Tomlin: Comedy with Bite." *New York Times*, 22 Sept. 1985: 3:1,4.

Forte, Jeanie. "Realism, Narrative, and the Feminist Playwright: A Problem of Reception." *Modern Drama* 32.1 (1989): 115-127.

Freud, Sigmund. *Collected Papers*, trans. Joan Riviere. 5 vols. New York: Basic Books, 1959.

Fried, John J. "Racism Awakens 'Stick Wife.'" Review of *The Stick Wife*, by Darrah Cloud. Los Angeles Theatre Center. *Press-Telegram* [Los Angeles, CA], 20 Jan. 1987: A6.

Frye, Joanne. *Living Stories, Telling Lives: Women and the Novel in Contemporary Experience*. Ann Arbor: University of Michigan Press, 1986.

Frye, Northrop. *Anatomy of Criticism: Four Essays*. 1957; reprint, Princeton, NJ: Princeton University Press, 1973.

Gagnier, Regina. "Between Women: A Cross-Class Analysis of Status and Anarchic Humor." In *Last Laughs: Perspectives on Women and Comedy*, ed. Regina Barreca. New York: Gordon and Breach, 1988. 135-148.

Gillespie, Patti. "Feminist Theatre: A Rhetorical Phenomenon." In *Women in American Theatre*, 2nd ed., ed. Helen Krich Chinoy and Linda Walsh Jenkins. New York: Theatre Communications Group, 1987. 278-286.

Gilligan, Carol. *In a Different Voice: Psychological Theory and Women's Development*. Cambridge, MA: Harvard University Press, 1982.

Göttner-Abendroth, Heide. "Nine Principles of a Matriarchal Aesthetic." In *Feminist Aesthetics,* ed. Gisela Ecker; trans. Harriet Anderson. Boston: Beacon Press, 1985.

Griffin, Leland. "A Dramatistic Theory of the Rhetoric of Movements." In *Critical Responses to Kenneth Burke,* ed. William H. Rueckert. Minneapolis: University of Minnesota Press, 1969.

Griffin, Susan. *Pornography and Silence: Culture's Revenge Against Nature.* New York: Harper and Row, 1981.

Gussow, Mel. "Stage: The Stick Wife, Klan Members in 1963." Review of *The Stick Wife,* by Darrah Cloud. Hartford Stage Company. *New York Times,* 25 Apr. 1987: I, 16.

———. "Women Playwrights: New Voices in the Theatre." *New York Times Magazine,* 1 May 1983: 22+.

Hooks, Bell. *Ain't I a Woman? Black Women and Feminism.* Boston: South End Press, 1981.

———. *Feminist Theory: From Margin to Center.* Boston: South End Press, 1984.

Hughes, Holly. Interview. *Hartford Courant,* 19 Sept. 1990: D1.

———. Personal interview. 8 Oct. 1989.

———. "The Well of Horniness." In *Out Front: Contemporary Gay and Lesbian Plays,* ed. Don Shewey. New York: Grove Press, 1988.

———, writer and performer. "World Without End." Directed by Kate Stafford. Bronson and Hutensky Theatre, Hartford. 7 Oct. 1989.

In the Boom Boom Room, by David Rabe (review). Anspacher Theatre, New York, *New York Times,* 5 Dec. 1974: 55.

Kauffmann, Stanley. "Suite and Sour." Review of *For Colored Girls,* by Ntozake Shange. Booth Theatre, New York. *New York Times,* 3 July 1976: 21.

Kerr, Walter. "Stage View: Are These Feminists Too Hard on Women?" Review of *Top Girls,* by Caryl Churchill. Public Theatre, New York. *New York Times,* 23 Jan. 1983: H3+.

Keyssar, Helene. "The Dramas of Caryl Churchill: The Politics of Possibility." *Massachusetts Review,* Spring 1983: 198-216.

―――. *Feminist Theatre: An Introduction to Plays of Contemporary British and American Women.* New York: Grove Press, 1985.

Kolodny, Annette. "Dancing Through the Minefield: Some Observations on the Theory, Practice, and Politics of Feminist Literary Criticism." In *The New Feminist Criticism: Essays on Women, Literature and Theory,* ed. Elaine Showalter. New York: Pantheon Books, 1985. 144-167.

Kroll, Jack. "Hollywood Wasteland." Review of *Hurlyburly,* by David Rabe. *Newsweek,* 2 July 1984: 65-67.

Lerner, Gerda. *Black Women in White America: A Documentary History.* New York: Random House, 1972.

―――. *The Creation of Patriarchy.* New York: Oxford University Press, 1986.

Levine, Joan B. "The Feminine Routine." *Journal of Communication* 26.3 (1976): 173-175.

Little, Judy. *Comedy and the Woman Writer: Woolf, Spark and Feminism.* Lincoln: University of Nebraska Press, 1983.

Malpede, Karen, ed. *Women in Theatre: Compassion and Hope.* New York: Harper and Row, 1985.

Martin, Linda, and Kerry Segrave. *Women in Comedy.* Secaucus, NJ: Citadel Press, 1984.

McGhee, Paul. "The Role of Laughter and Humor in Growing Up Female." In *Becoming Female: Perspectives in Women and Comedy,* ed. Claire B. Kopp, New York: Plenum Press, 1979.

Meyer, Michael, comp. *Ibsen on File.* Writers on File Series. London: Methuen, 1985.

Miller, Jean Baker. *Toward a New Psychology of Women.* 2nd ed. Boston: Beacon Press, 1986.

Mitgang, Herbert. "Stage: Revised Version of 'Boom Boom Room.'" Review of *In the Boom Boom Room,* by David Rabe. South Street Theater, New York. *New York Times,* 22 Dec. 1985: 1:59.

Moore, Honor. "Woman Alone, Women Together." In *Women in American Theatre.* 2nd ed., eds. Helen Krich Chinoy and Linda Walsh Jenkins. New York: Theatre Communications Group, 1987. 186-191.

Morgan, Robin. *The Anatomy of Freedom.* Garden City, NY: Anchor Press, 1984.

Natalle, Elizabeth J. *Feminist Theatre: A Study in Persuasion.* Metuchen: Scarecrow Press, 1985.

Norman, Marsha. *Getting Out.* New York: Dramatists Play Service, 1979.

————. *'Night, Mother.* New York: Hill and Wang, 1983.

————, screenwriter. *'Night, Mother* (film). Dir. Tom Moore. With Geraldine Fitzgerald and Sissy Spacek. Universal Studios, 1986.

Rabe, David. ". . .And as Rabe Sees Hollywood." Interview with Helen Dudar. *New York Times,* 28 June 1984, 3:13.

————. *Hurlyburly.* New York: Grove Press, 1985.

————. *In the Boom Boom Room.* New York: Alfred A. Knopf, 1975.

————. Interview. *New York Times,* 24 Nov. 1973: 22.

————. Interview. *New York Times,* 12 May 1976: 34.

Rabuzzi, Kathryn Allen. *The Sacred and the Feminine: Toward a Theology of Housework.* New York: Seabury Press, 1982.

Radway, Janice A. *Reading the Romance: Women, Patriarchy and Popular Literature.* Chapel Hill: University of North Carolina Press, 1984.

Reinelt, Janelle. "Beyond Brecht: Britain's New Feminist Drama." *Theatre Journal,* May 1986: 154-163.

Rich, Frank. Review of *The Brothers,* by Kathleen Collins. *New York Times,* 6 Apr. 1982, 3:13.

————. "Stage: Caryl Churchill's 'Top Girls' at the Public." Review of *Top Girls,* by Caryl Churchill. Public Theatre, New York. *New York Times,* 29 Dec. 1982: C17.

————. "Theater: Hurlyburly." Review of *Hurlyburly,* by David Rabe. *New York Times,* 22 June 1984, 3:3.

Schickel, Richard. "Failing Words." Review of *Hurlyburly,* by David Rabe. Promenade Theatre, New York. *Time,* 2 July 1984: 86-87.

Schroeder, Patricia R. "Locked Behind the Proscenium: Feminist Strategies in *Getting Out* and *My Sister in This House.*" *Modern Drama* 32.1 (1989): 104-114.

Shange, Ntozake. *For Colored Girls Who Have Considered Suicide When the Rainbow is Enuf.* New York: Macmillan, 1977.

Showalter, Elaine. *A Literature of Their Own: British Women Novelists From Brontë to Lessing.* Princeton, NJ: Princeton University Press, 1977.

Simon, John. "War Games." Review of *Hurlyburly,* by David Rabe. Promenade Theatre, New York. *New York,* 16 July 1984: 42-43.

Smith, Barbara. "Toward a Black Feminist Criticism." In *All the Women Are White, All the Blacks Are Men, But Some of Us Are Brave: Black Women's Studies,* eds. Gloria T. Hull, Patricia Bell Scott, and Barbara Smith. Old Westbury, NY: Feminist Press, 1982.

Snyder, Carol. "Reading the Language of the Dinner Party." *Women's Art Journal* 1.2 (1980-1981): 30-34.

Spacks, Patricia Meyer. "Austen's Laughter." In *Last Laughs:*

Perspectives on Women and Comedy, ed. Regina Barreca. New York: Gordon and Breach, 1989.

Wagner, Jane. *The Search for Signs of Intelligent Life in the Universe.* New York: Harper and Row, 1986.

Walker, Alice. "One Child of One's Own: A Meaningful Digression Within the Work(s)—An Excerpt." In *All the Women Are White, All the Blacks Are Men, But Some of us Are Brave: Black Women's Studies,* Eds. Gloria T. Hull, Patricia Bell Scott, and Barbara Smith. Old Westbury, NY: Feminist Press, 1982.

Willeford, William. *The Fool and His Sceptre.* Evanston, IL: Northwestern University Press, 1969.

Zillman, Dolf, and S. Holly Stocking. "Putdown Humor." *Journal of Communication* 26.3 (1976): 173-175.

Index